PUB WALKS

DAVID HANCOCK

Ensign

First published in 1992
by **Ensign Publications**
a division of Hampshire Books Ltd.,
2 Redcar Street
Southampton SO1 5LL

a b c d

ISBN 185455 084 5

Winchester \ Basingstoke

Publisher: David Graves
Maps: Jack Street
Cover Photo: Terry Heathcote
Book photos: Bonita Toms
Cover Design: The Design Lab
Text pages: The Precinct Press
Printers: Romsey Printing Co., Chandlers Ford

Also available in this series
Pub Walks in the New Forest
Pub Walks on the Isle of Wight (1993)
Pub Walks in and around the New Forest (1993)
Pub Walks around Salisbury and Andover (1993)
Pub Walks around Bournemouth and Poole (1993)
Pub Walks around Portsmouth & the South Downs
Pub Walks around Southampton and Central Hampshire

Walk	· CONTENTS ·	Page

· INTRODUCTION ·

This part of Hampshire offers a diverse range of landscapes and scenery for the walker to explore. From the tracks that traverse the rolling chalk downland of the Hampshire 'highlands' to the peaceful pathways that follow the tranquil valleys and waters of the county's chalk streams — the Test and Itchen. This selection of 20 circular walks take you through some of the best scenery that this area has to offer, covering distances of between 4 and 8 miles. Comprehensive route descriptions are accompanied by a precise sketch map and a section outlining historical details about the villages, the surrounding area and places of interest on each walk.

The perfect complement to a three hour rural ramble that has stimulated a healthy appetite and a parched throat is the sight of an unspoilt country pub. Each walk radiates from a pub and it is assumed you will want to enjoy their hospitality before or after your walk. Most publicans are happy for walkers to use their car parks, but it is best to ask permission before leaving your car. All the pubs have been visited in order to collate the detailed information concerning opening and bar food times, type of food, range of ales and whether children and dogs are welcome. Do remember that pubs are liable to change hands or close at short notice.

Hampshire County Council rights of way and recreation department endeavour to upkeep all the paths, adding new signs and replacing stiles, and it must be said that the majority of paths are well-maintained and waymarked and as a consequence are walked on a regular basis. A common complaint from ramblers concerns landowners who do not restore footpaths after ploughing or obscuring them with crops. However, the Rights of Way Act which came into force in 1990, now requires the landowner to reinstate footpaths within 24 hours of a disturbance or two weeks if the disturbance is the first time for that crop. If you have any problems while out walking you should contact the rights of way officer at Hampshire County Council.

Most of the routes are on country paths which may be muddy, so stout footwear is advisable. Remember to carry a light waterproof and a walking stick, which is useful for clearing any overgrown paths and for checking the stability of the ground ahead. Always remember the country code — fasten all gates, keep dogs under control and always on a lead where there are livestock, do not damage property, keep to public rights of way, do not dig up wild plants and take your litter home.

Finally, we hope you enjoy exploring the depths of the Hampshire countryside as much as we did while researching these walks.

DAVID HANCOCK
November, 1992

Ancient tracks and towpaths around historic Winchester

WALK 1
Up to **4 hours**
6 $^1/_2$ miles
Walk begins page 7

Background to the walk

Winchester, ancient capital of Wessex and England, lies steeped in history in the heart of the Hampshire countryside. First settled in the Iron Age and influenced by royalty since the 7th century the city has some remarkable architectural treasures. The Great Hall is the only surviving remnant of Winchester Castle built by Henry III and later demolished by Cromwell. The magnificent cathedral built in the 11th century and remodelled in the 14th century has the longest nave in Europe and the burial place for ancient kings and more recent notables.

To the south and east of the Cathedral Close beyond Kingsgate arch, one of the two surviving medieval city gateways, lies Winchester College and a maze of narrow lanes lined with attractive houses. The Wykeham Arms, with its fine bowed doors is situated on the corner of two of these charming streets, Kingsgate Street and Canon Street. The 250-year-old inn looks out towards the tiny St Swithun's church situated above Kingsgate arch, one of the few churches in England in such an unusual position.

College Street has much to offer the visitor. Jane Austen took lodgings at number 8 in May 1817 and died there a few weeks later. She is buried in the cathedral. The house is not open but a plaque records her stay. Further along the street is the entrance to Winchester College, founded in 1382 by William of Wykeham, Bishop of Winchester, and the oldest public school in England.

Maps
*Landranger 1:50,000
Sheet 185
Pathfinder 1:25,000
Sheet SU 42/52
Map Reference of
Start/Finish SU481290*

How to get there
Parking at the Wykeham Arms is extremely limited due to the narrow streets. It is best to park at one of the long stay public car parks in the town: Chesil Street, Tower Street, Abbey Road, Worthy Lane or behind the railway station. Then on foot from the Butter Cross, situated in the pedestrianised High Street, go through the narrow passageway into The Square. Proceed ahead past the City Museum along the main tree-lined path to the cathedral doors, then follow the path to your right beneath the buttresses into the Cathedral Close. Keep to the roadway, leaving the Close by St

Swithun's Gate and turn left under Kingsgate arch. The Wykeham Arms is directly ahead of you in Kingsgate Street.

Pub facilities
The Wykeham Arms

Tucked away between the College and the cathedral the 250 year old 'Wyk', as it is affectionately called, prides itself for the excellent quality food served in its characterful bars. In winter, three log fires warm the six separate areas, all of which are decorated with fine old prints and collections of hats, mugs or books. The main bar is furnished with redundant college desks, the others with a mix of settles, farmhouse kitchen chairs and pine, candle-lit tables. Well-conditioned Eldridge Pope real ales include Dorchester 'boys' Bitter, Hardy Country, Royal Oak and the dark Porter ale. Twenty wines are available by the glass to compliment the imaginative dishes chalked up on the daily-changing blackboard menu. Lunchtime choices include sandwiches, soups, pâtés, cauliflower cheese,

Beyond the barrier at the far end of College Street is the Bishop's House, where the Bishop of Winchester resides. It is the surviving wing of a palace built in 1684 and overlooks the ruins of the 12th century Wolvesey Castle.

Set in the wide, lush meadows beside the River Itchen is the Hospital of St Cross. It was founded by Bishop Henry of Blois in 1136 and is the oldest charitable institution in the country. The original provision was for the housing of thirteen old men and free dinners every day for one-hundred other poor men. The 'Wayfarers Dole' of bread and ale may still be claimed from the Porters Lodge.

The Clarendon Way passes through St Cross and along the banks of the River Itchen into Winchester, at the end of the 25 mile long-distance walk that links the cathedral towns of Salisbury and Winchester. Named after the former medieval palace which it passes on the outskirts of Salisbury it generally follows the route of the ancient Roman road between the two cities.

Across the meadows from St Cross is the village of Compton which consists of a long street leading nowhere, lined with pleasant houses and a thatched barn. Its name simply means 'a village in a combe' and that is exactly what it is, tucked down in a dry chalk valley. All Saints church is unusual as enlargements to the original Norman features in 1905 included adding a new nave and chancel.

Between Winchester and Southampton the Itchen Navigation was established in the 17th century, using the natural course of the river for much of its length. It was used to transport heavy cargoes such as coal in horse-drawn barges from the docks in Southampton to Wharf Hill in Winchester. The last barges ceased operating in 1869. Fifteen locks were built along its length and the remains of most of these are visible along the Itchen Way which follows the towpath.

Further up the Itchen valley near Winchester, the old navigation passes beneath the most prominent landmark around the city, St

Catherine's Hill. The Iron Age Hill Fort on top of the hill has a massive rampart and ditch and was occupied between 500 and 100BC. Within the fort defences, beneath the clump of beech trees are the Norman remains of St Catherine's Chapel. To the north of the trees is a 17th century turf-cut maze, known as the 'Mizmaze'.

Walk 1.

Distance: *Allow up to four hours for this six-and-a-half mile walk, longer if planning to visit the various historic buildings in Winchester.*

From the Wykeham Arms turn left towards Kingsgate arch and follow the road round into College Street. Pass the house where Jane Austen died and the cobbled entrance to the 14th century college on your right, then shortly, at the road barrier turn right along College Walk. Behind you is the Bishop's House and the ruins of Wolvesey Castle. Where the road turns sharp left, turn right along a gravel track waymarked 'St Cross via the water meadows'. This is the beginning of the Clarendon Way, a long distance walk which links

cottage pie or pasta carbonara. Creative evening dishes range from venison casserole and pan-fried pigeon breast with a blackcurrant and cassis sauce to breast of chicken in filo pastry. Delicious home made puddings include cinnamon and apple crumble, rhubarb fool and treacle and walnut tart. Food can be ordered between 1200-1400 and 1830-2100 (except Sundays). The bar is open from 1100-2300 weekdays (usual times on Sundays). Summer eating and drinking can be enjoyed in the rear walled garden or on the sheltered patio. Children under 14 are not allowed in the bars.

Winchester and Salisbury. When you reach the private entrance to the college turn left through a metal gate onto a gravel path, with the college playing fields on your right and the clear waters of the River Itchen to your left. St Catherine's Hill with its Iron Age Fort and distinctive clump of beech trees dominates the water meadow scene away to your left.

After half a mile your route crosses Garnier Road and continues along another gravel path to the right of a pumping station, with streams on both sides. Pass through a kissing gate and cross a concrete sluice into lush meadowland with the 12th century church and hospital of St Cross ahead of you. At the wall turn right signed to the hospital and shortly join the private lane to the hospital, following it out to the main St Cross road. Here you turn right, then cross over into Mead Road and proceed uphill to a footbridge across the Southampton to London railway. Once over the railway, you turn left at the Clarendon Way logo and walk gradually uphill along an established sunken pathway, known as Whiteshute Lane. At breaks in the thick hedgerow you can enjoy fine vistas back into the Itchen valley to St Cross. Eventually drop down to and cross Badger Farm Road following the waymarked route along a wide chalk trackway.

At a crossroads of tracks, with excellent views of St Cross and the rolling hills beyond the Itchen valley to your left and ahead to Yew Hill, proceed straight on along a wide track beside a hedge with an open field to your right. The old trackway gradually descends into the valley ahead passing between a line of beech trees, later giving way to fir trees on your left and a hawthorn hedge to your right. The track soon bears round to the left with the curve of the hill and becomes a metalled lane through the village of Compton. Pass the quaint All Saints church and the primary school and cross the busy road, which links Winchester to Compton and the A33, into Place Lane.

Walk past Stoney Drive Farm on your right, then, where the lane splits bear right onto a track and shortly pass under the A33 Winchester bypass,

following the track around to your left to a small wooden gate. We found the deafening noise of the traffic here quite unpleasant and irritating, so we quickly strode out through the tunnel under the railway, keeping right at the far end onto a defined pathway, in anticipation of the peaceful waters of the Itchen navigation ahead. Ignore the waymarked path on your left to 'St Cross', proceed ahead to cross two footbridges, then a plank, beyond which you emerge out onto the banks of the Itchen navigation at what remains of Compton Lock. Pause for a moment, to savour the tranquil watermeadow scene with Twyford church looming above the trees ahead. Cross the footbridge over the navigation and turn left along the east bank.

The pathway along the navigation is part of the Itchen Way, a 27-mile designated walk that follows the course of the river from its source just south of Cheriton, to where it enters Southampton Water at Weston Shore. In half a mile cross the footbridge over an overflow channel and shortly, the River Itchen will come into view on the right. The path soon passes between the two waterways and crosses a sluice which discharges water from the navigation into a small pond-like area to form the lower part of the River Itchen. Remain on the path beside the navigation bearing right where the river joins the old silted up navigation and follow the path out onto the B3335, opposite the entrance to Hockley Golf Course.

Cross over the road and follow the footway to the Hockley traffic lights and the workings of the proposed M3 extension. At present their are no diversions here, but when the extension is completed the Hockley to Twyford road will be moved slightly and will pass under the motorway. Once on the other side, the footpath will be directed right to join the existing pathway along the old navigation. At the moment one must cross over the dual carriageway at the lights, taking great care via the central island. Once over this busy stretch of road you turn right onto a tarmac footway, which shortly gives way to what can be a muddy pathway under a disused railway.

Remain on this sheltered path between the dual carriageway on the right and the old navigation on your left to a tunnel under the road, beyond which is a stile and a pathway up the side of St Catherine's Hill. This is a pleasant diversion for the views across Winchester from the top are quite superb. Back on the main route along the navigation, take the lower path beside the water's edge to Tun Bridge and Garnier Road. Here you cross the road, continuing along the towpath with a playing field to your right. Pass in front of a group of modern dwellings and shortly bear right to join a lane. Turn left, pass the college rowing club on your left and at the end turn left into College Walk. Cross over the river, following the road round a sharp right-hand bend to rejoin the outward route back along College Street to the Wykeham Arms.

A walk from *The Brushmakers Arms* at Upham

WALK 2
Up to **4 hours**
7 ¹/₂ miles
Walk begins page 12

Background to the walk

Upham is comprised of Lower Upham which straggles along the busy B-road, and the main village quietly situated a mile away amidst country lanes. Many 18th and 19th century brick cottages and houses line the semi-circle of a lane that links the church to the Brushmakers Arms and creates the true heart of this attractive village. A classic duck pond completes the scene. Until the 19th century the village was the centre of a flourishing brushmaking industry and the evidence of this craft survives locally only in the pub name, the pub having once been a brushmakers shop.

During the Civil War Cromwell's troops often used churches to stable their horses, and past church registers at the church of the Blessed Mary include an entry concerning the cleaning out of the chancel after occupation by Roundhead cavalry. The present church is Victorian, except for its short, chequered brick tower which was constructed in the 18th century.

The poet Edward Young, author of 'Night Thoughts' was born in the village in 1683 when his father, a royal chaplain, was rector for the village. Young is credited with the remark 'Procrastination is the thief of time'.

One of the largest zoological parks in Britain lies just west of Upham and makes a pleasant diversion on this walk. Marwell is run by a charity and has for the past twenty years been dedicated to the conservation of endangered animals. There

Maps
Landranger 1:50,000 Sheet 185
Pathfinder 1:25,000 Sheet SU 42/52
Map Reference of Start/Finish SU540206

How to get there
From Basingstoke take the M3 to Winchester. From Winchester follow the A333 south through St Cross and turn right a quarter of mile beyond the Bell Inn to the Hockley traffic lights. Cross over the A33 onto the B3335 through Twyford and keep left at the junction with the A335 through Colden Common. At Fishers Pond, turn left onto the B2177 towards Bishop's Waltham and after two-and-a-half miles turn left, opposite the B3037 to Fair Oak onto a lane signed to Upham. Hampshire Bus or Gemini Travel service 69 connecting Winchester to Portsmouth via Bishop's Waltham and Fareham

are over 100 acres of parkland surrounding Marwell Hall. The Hall, built in 1816 on the site of an earlier house once owned by the brother of Jane Seymour, the third wife of Henry VIII, now houses an education centre. The zoo is open every day except Christmas Day.

The hilltop village of Owslebury, the second highest in Hampshire has the odd timber-framed and thatched cottage, but is predominantly modern in the style of its buildings. This cannot be said however, for the Church of St Andrew which dates from the 13th century and was altered on several occasions during the 17th century. Evidence of this is found on the west side of the tower which has a stone bearing the date 1676. It has been described rather unkindly as having been 'tinkered up by successive vicars with more zeal than artistic taste'. Inside, the iron pillars supporting the aisles were panelled in wood in 1956, and a serpent, a primitive wind instrument, used in the church band in 1840, is on display.

Visitors to Owslebury are often perplexed as to how to pronounce its name and how the name was derived. The 'local' way is to rhyme the first two syllables with 'jostle', thus pronouncing it 'Ostlebury'. According to place-name authorities the village was most likely a fortified stronghold belonging to someone called Osla.

Walk 2.

Distance: *Allow four hours for this walk of about seven-and-a-half miles.*

We parked the car on the lane beside the village pond, as parking is difficult on the narrow lane outside the pub. From the pond follow the lane left, the Brushmakers is visible just up the lane on your right. Pass the church of Blessed Mary with its two big yew trees guarding the gate and turn right along another lane, towards the fingerpost waymarking your route left ahead. Go through the gate beside 'Freshfields' and cross the field, keep-

stops at the Alma Inn in Lower Upham from which it is a mile along the lane to the main village. The walk can be started and finished at Marwell Zoo by alighting service 69 at the zoo entrance.

Pub facilities
The Brushmakers

is a pub with a fascinating history. The building is over 600-years old. It is recorded that Cromwell stayed here during the Civil War while his men were garrisoned up the road. Since then it has been a brushmaker's workshop and a pub and was once the meeting place for brushmaker's from all over Hampshire, when the craft was at its height. The inn is well-documented for its resident ghosts and the landlord will recount his experiences if asked. Main bar is the oldest part of the inn and features a low, partly-beamed ceiling, comfortable cushioned wall benches, wheel-backed chairs and dark wood tables. The pub is a free house and serves draught Bass and Morland Old Masters on hand pump. Bar food is

ing to the right of a lone hawthorn bush to a stile. Bear half-left across the arable field towards the first tree along the fence to your left, where you will join a grassy path along a mixed hedgerow, which descends into a small wood.

Emerge from the wood and proceed downhill across another arable field, where you should find the path well-defined through the crops. Pass through a copse to a stile, then head uphill across the next field to the stile visible in the line of trees ahead. Turn left along the field edge, then in twenty yards you turn right uphill, along a wide grassy farm track between crops. It is hard to believe that away to your left are the built-up areas of Eastleigh and Southampton, as the view encompasses a landscape of arable fields and trees. The air quality was exceptional when we walked this path and we could see in the far distance the rolling downland on the Isle of Wight.

Where the trackway bears left towards farm buildings, keep ahead to a gravel track where you turn left, then immediately right into woodland onto a track signed 'no vehicles'. Your route now follows the main track to the left, which we found to be quite muddy. A couple of signs clearly state that the woods around you are private, so keep to the track and shortly emerge into an open field. Turn left, following the edge of the wood through a gap into another field. At the end of the wood, disregard the wide grassy path to your left, keep ahead towards the fence and cross the stile on your left. Bear right along the field edge with Marwell House visible through the trees to your right. Climb another stile and remain following the right-hand edge of the field towards some houses and a further stile, over which you turn right onto a wide grassy path. Just before the houses ahead of you, bear right to join a gravel driveway and follow the HCC official footpath diversion along the drive, passing the entrance to Marwell Farmhouse to a lane.

Turn right, shortly passing the turning to Baybridge on your right. Just after the left-hand

popular, especially the Sunday roasts. Booking advisable. Standard menu supplemented with specials — steak pie, peppered steak and chicken, lemon and coriander. Other dishes — lasagne, curries, a range of vegetarian dishes and ploughmans. Food available lunchtimes from 1200-1400 and Wednesday-Saturday in the evenings between 1830-2100. The pub is open from 1100-1430 and 1830-2300, from 1900 Monday and Tuesday. Children welcome in the room away from the bar. Dogs allowed in bar on a lead, but not in garden.

The Ship Inn, Owslebury

A fine downland village inn, dating from 1681 with characterful bars and a reputation for good bar food and well-kept Marstons ales. Food is served Monday to Saturday 1200-1400 and 1900-2100, (2130 on Fridays and Saturdays). Children welcome in the family room or large garden which has an excellent play area. Walkers may park their cars here if they are using the pub.

St. Andrew's church, Owslebury — 'tinkered up by successive vicars with more zeal than artistic taste'

bend, turn left onto a gravel track leading to the padlocked perimeter fence of Marwell Zoo. Here you follow the waymarked bridleway to your left along the fence. The narrow pathway soon gives way to a wide, extremely wet and muddy bridleway, churned up by the regular passage of horses. Your route now runs parallel with the zoo's perimeter fence through woodland, crossing one of its entrance driveways back into the wood, before emerging along the right-hand edge of a field to a lane. Here you turn right onto a wide pathway through the trees and cross over the main entrance road to the zoo.

You now join another equally muddy bridleway which passes between the zoo car park and woodland. Walkers have created narrow paths that weave through the woodland parallel to the quagmire of a bridleway. Shortly, cross a track at the end of the car park back into woodland, then proceed straight across at a junction of paths into a woodland, with a red sign indicating that it is 'zoo property'. On reaching a fork in the path, with an open field in front of you, bear right along a muddy path which soon bears right and becomes a tree-lined route between arable fields. You now gradually climb for three-quarters of a mile, before bearing right along a track to a lane where you turn right passing Boyes Farm and the Ship Inn

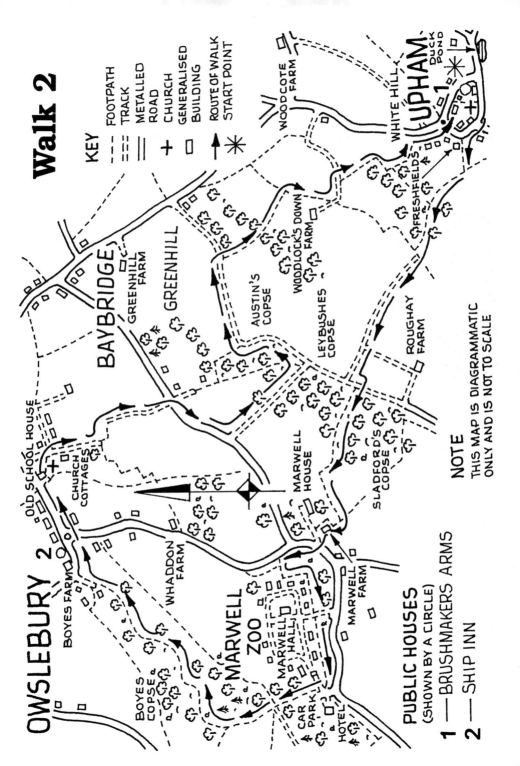

The Brushmakers Arms

on your left, into the village of Owslebury.

Walk along the lane through the village and turn right in front of the Old School House and enter St Andrews churchyard. We found the church locked due to the 'prohibitively high cost of insuring most unlocked churches', according to a statement on the door. Those wishing to explore inside can acquire the key at a house called The Granary. A fingerpost directs you through the churchyard, down a few steps onto a gravel track where you turn right, to follow the waymarked path past Church Cottages. The track soon gives way to a narrow path between hedges, downhill to a gate.

Turn left along the hedge, downhill into the bottom of a dry chalk valley and proceed uphill to join a grass-and-gravel track, which bears right with open views. Descend to a gate flanked by a stile and turn right along a quiet lane. Follow the lane for about a quarter of a mile before turning left along an established trackway, which soon takes you through thick woodland. When you reach a T-junction of tracks turn left, following the gravel track around the edge of the woodland, soon to veer right away from the wood. At the first tree on your right go through a gap, either side of a wooden stake and proceed ahead alongside the hedge on your left. Pass through the narrow wood ahead of you, cross a stile and keep to the right-hand edge of a large field, which affords open views southwards.

In the far corner of the field, make your way into the field ahead, where you follow its right-hand edge. Cross a track, walk along the right edge of another field and turn left onto the track leading to the farm buildings away to your right. Just before the woodland on your left, bear off right onto a defined path, downhill across an arable field and go through the narrow strip of woodland ahead. Continue across the arable field that now confronts you, heading uphill to the trees, just to the right of the left-hand corner. A narrow path takes you into the wood where you immediately turn left onto an established path which brings you out to a lane. Bear right, uphill into Upham, turning left at the junction ahead and follow the lane back to the Brushmakers Arms and the village pond.

Hedged tracks and paths from Braishfield

Background to the walk

The main heart of the village of Braishfield consists of a pond, a few attractive thatched cottages, mixed in with some modern houses and the interesting church of All Saints, built in 1885 by the Victorian architect Butterfield. He was famous in his time for the use of coloured bricks in his buildings and this shows in the decorative spirelet that the church displays. It also has an elaborately fitted chancel with wall paintings. It was in Braishfield, back in 1971 that the site of the oldest building in England was discovered. A mesolithic house, probably some 8,500 years old was discovered by archaeologist Michael O'Malley after he had unearthed a series of flints. His work won him a BBC 'Chronicle' award in 1979.

The village is also known to have at least two ghosts; one, an Edwardian lady is seen looking for her lost jewels, while the second apparition is of a human form seen in the branches of an old yew tree, near a deserted farmhouse.

Perched high above the picturesque Test valley is the attractive village of Michelmersh. The older, northern-most part of the parish comprises thatched cottages, larger Georgian and early-Victorian houses which line the narrow lanes that lead to the fascinating church of St Mary. The church is best known for its unusual weatherboarded, detached tower, its timber-framed interior is thought to be 15th century. The rest of the church is flint, much of it dating from 1847 when it was extensively restored. There is

Maps
Landranger 1:50,000 Sheet 185. Pathfinder 1:25,000 Sheet SU 22/ 32 Map Reference of Start/Finish SU372250

How to get there
From Basingstoke take M3 to Winchester. From Winchester head south-west on the A3090 towards Romsey, passing the prison and the hospital as you leave the town centre. Follow the signs to Hursley and Romsey. Beyond Hursley the A3090 merges with the A31 and passes through the village of Ampfield. Take the first turning on your right past the Potters Heron Hotel, signed to Hilliers Arboretum and Braishfield. At the crossroads beyond the Arboretum entrance turn right and follow the lane for a mile, turning first left after passing the Wheatsheaf towards Michelmersh and the

however, a big 12th century chancel and some interesting memorials. One chancel window has remnants of a cross-legged effigy of a Crusader knight with a stag at his feet, thought to be from about 1320. A memorial to Tristram Fantleroy (1538) is probably the earliest example in Hampshire with detached kneeling figures.

The field south of the church is called Agincourt Field and is said to have been the scene of an historic event on 16th July 1415. More than 600 knights and archers of the English army camped here before sailing to France and the Battle of Agincourt.

At Old Michelmersh Farm opposite the church, a very old and unusual five-bayed, weatherboarded granary can be seen. It has a hipped and tiled roof, rests on staddle stones and is thought to be the largest of its kind in Hampshire.

Walk 3.

Distance: *Allow three-and-a-half hours for this six mile walk.*

On leaving the Newport Inn turn right along the lane into the village and turn left at the T-junction down to the war memorial, a short distance ahead of you. Here you turn right, signed 'Winchester', then bear left at the pond at the fingerpost waymarking your route towards the church. The lane bears left to All Saints church at 'Long Barn' and is well worth the short diversion for its decorative spirelet and its tranquil setting. Having visited the church, return to 'Long Barn' and turn left along a narrow lane. Disregard the waymarked path on your right, keep ahead towards 'Meade Hill', the lane soon giving way to a gravel track. When you reach a metal gate with a board stating 'private, appointments only' turn left onto a signed footpath between a hedgerow and a wire fence, which takes you around a collection of farm buildings and machinery. Ignore the stile and fingerpost to your right and shortly pass between

Newport Inn. It is best to park at the hall next to the church, which can be reached by turning first right beyond the Wheatsheaf at the war memorial, then bear left by the pond at the sign directing you to the church. Hampshire Bus service 66 from Winchester connects at Romsey with Gemini Travel service 35 to Braishfield.

Pub facilities
The Newport Inn
This unassuming brick-built pub was originally two cottages back in the 1860s, the front half being added on in 1905 when it became a pub. A certain rustic, old fashioned charm pervades at the Newport for it is a true traditional local and probably looks exactly as it did 50 years ago when the present landlady took over the pub. Inside, there is a well-worn feel to the two, simply furnished bars; the large 'Tap' room with its original frosted glass windows has a lino floor, an old piano strewn with magazines and books, plush wall bench seats and stools around cane and wooden

tables and two open fires warm the room in winter. The other bar is carpeted and has a real mix of simple furniture. The place to sit on fine days is in the sheltered front garden complete with rabbits and roaming chickens and enjoy the excellent Gales beers — HSB and Butser Bitter — that are available. Food is limited to ploughman's and a range of sandwiches which are huge and excellent value-for-money. Children are not allowed in the pub but there is plenty to amuse them in the garden. Opening times are 1000-1430 and 1800-2300 on weekdays and the usual pub hours (1200-1500 and 1900-2230) on Sundays.

two houses, then along a line of beech trees to a lane.

Turn right, proceed ahead when you reach a crossroads and bear left in front of a vineyard onto a waymarked bridleway which takes you uphill past Braishfield Manor on your left. Remain on the grass-cum-gravel track, following it round to the left on reaching an isolated house, then keep left at the bridleway fingerpost to join another trackway. From here you can enjoy the open views across the wooded Hampshire landscape towards Romsey, Southampton and the New Forest.

Bear left at the next fingerpost, your route still following a wide track with a tall tree-hedge to your right and open views away to the left. On reaching a metal gate just after a right-hand bend, turn left onto a waymarked narrow bridleway between high, thick hedges which leads you to a quiet lane. Turn right along the lane and bear left onto a signed grass-cum-gravel track where the lane bears sharp right. You will now pass between hazel and oak trees along the edge of a small wood, shortly to emerge onto an old established routeway, with open views to your left and a thick mixed hedgerow on your right.

This undulating grassy track soon gives way to a gravel farm road, where you disregard the arrowed path and stile on your right to follow the wide hedge-lined track round a sharp left-hand bend and eventually to a T-junction of tracks. Turn right, your route now passes through Michelmersh Manor Farm. Where the track bears right in front of a house, keep left and climb the stile situated to the right of the driveway to a bungalow and follow

the narrow path between the two properties to another stile. Cross the stile and follow the yellow arrow head directing you across the field ahead, along the remains of an old hedgerow. Climb the stile in front of you and pass through a small copse to a further stile flanking a metal gate. Keep to the right-hand hedge and soon you will have your first view of the fine Norman church of St Mary's in Michelmersh *(pictured above)*, with its unusual 15th century detached wooden tower.

Cross the stile in the fence ahead of you and walk through the churchyard — which is often grazed by sheep — on a defined grassy path to a wooden gate. Pause for a while here, as we did, to savour the peaceful location that the church enjoys, especially the views across the Test valley and peruse the excellent notes available in the church, detailing its history from the 12th century.

From the porch of the church, follow the wooden fence on your left to the corner, pass through a small wooden swing gate and bear half-left across the field to a stile in the hedgerow. You now join a narrow path between wire fences lined with trees, pass through a wooden walk-through stile and walk behind the back gardens of the houses in Michelmersh on a wide grassy path. When you reach a garage on your left, proceed ahead along a gravel track beside a line of poplars to a wooden swing-gate, situated beside a red-painted metal gate.

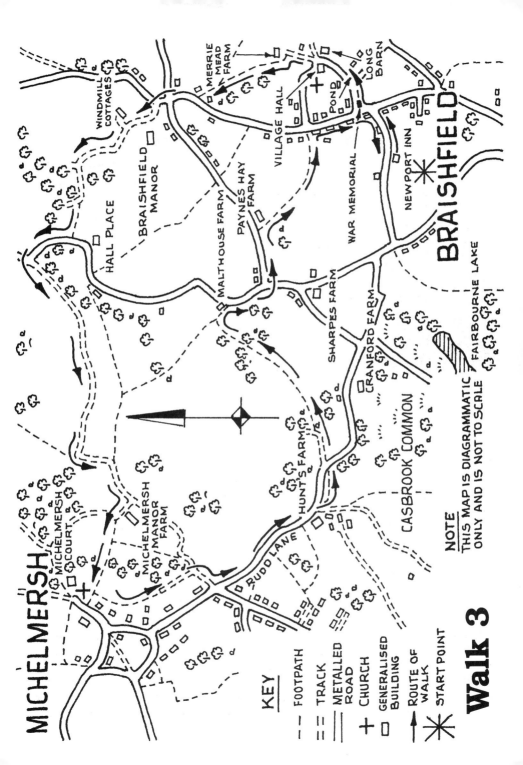

MICHELMERSH

BRAISHFIELD

WINDMILL COTTAGES

MERRIE MEAD FARM

LONG BARN

VILLAGE HALL

POND

BRAISHFIELD MANOR

HALL PLACE

MALTHOUSE FARM

PAYNES HAY FARM

WAR MEMORIAL

NEWPORT INN

MICHELMERSH COURT

MICHELMERSH MANOR FARM

RUDD LANE

HUNT'S FARM

SHARPES FARM

CRANFORD FARM

CASBROOK COMMON

FAIRBOURNE LAKE

NOTE
THIS MAP IS DIAGRAMMATIC ONLY AND IS NOT TO SCALE

KEY

– – FOOTPATH

= = TRACK

||| METALLED ROAD

+ CHURCH

▢ GENERALISED BUILDING

→ ROUTE OF WALK

✳ START POINT

Walk 3

Shortly, turn right onto a metalled lane, then on reaching a crossroads you turn left into Rudd Lane, passing a series of brick cottages on your left. Remain on the lane, eventually passing Hunts Farm on your right and keep left at the next junction disregarding the waymarked route to your right towards the Redland Tile Works. At the top of a short incline, bear right at the fingerpost directing you onto a pathway along the bank, parallel to the narrow lane. Take care as you cross the entrance to quarry workings and shortly turn right back onto the lane.

In twenty yards, cross the lane and climb the stile on your left, where your route is waymarked by a yellow arrow. Follow a track to where it bears left to a green-painted gate. Here, proceed ahead across a small concrete bridge over a drainage channel onto a well-defined and signed path through scrubland, gradually climbing uphill along a tree-lined hedge to a stile. Your route follows the right-hand fence before descending to a metal gate and a wide trackway through a narrow stretch of woodland. When you emerge from the trees bear half-right across the field ahead of you, towards a house and climb the stile in the far right-hand corner. Follow a narrow hedged pathway to a gravel drive near some old sheds, here you bear left to a lane.

Turn right and follow the quiet lane to a T-junction where you turn left passing a magnificent timber-framed, thatched cottage on your left. Beyond an old barn look out for a waymarked path across a stile in the hedge to your right. Follow the left-hand fence, then across the corner of the field to a stile and pathway leading into woodland. Your route takes you through a uniformly planted area of poplar trees to a stile, then along the left-hand edge of a field to another stile. Climb this and go through the small wooden gate beyond, keeping right along the edge of a garden, following the yellow arrow onto a driveway which leads you down to a lane. Turn right into Braishfield village centre, pass the war memorial on your left and rejoin the outward route back to your car and the Newport Inn.

Exploring the Test Valley around Horsebridge

WALK 4
Upto **4 $^1/_2$ hours**
7 $^1/_2$ miles
Walk begins page 25

Background to the walk

The River Test is one of the great English rivers, renowned around the world for its game fishing, particularly trout. For much of its length the Test is not one stream but two, three or four separate channels with clear, sparkling water sometimes merging to create broad, bright shallows.

There are few footpaths across the river or along the valley, as much of the river bank is privately owned and reserved for expensive and exclusive fishing. It was not until the creation of the long distance walks, the Test Way and more recently the Clarendon Way that the Test valley — especially between Stockbridge and Romsey — has been accessible to walkers. The Test Way traverses Hampshire from south to north and for two-thirds of its length follows the valley of the River Test while the Clarendon Way links the cathedral cities of Salisbury and Winchester and crosses the Test near King's Somborne.

Between Lower Brook and Fullerton the Test Way follows the disused Test Valley Railway, affectionately known as the 'Sprat and Winkle' line, a distance of 10 miles. It was built in 1865, replacing the old canal that ran between Redbridge and Andover, but closed during the Beeching era in 1964. The old railway station at Horsebridge has been preserved more or less as it was, complete with waiting room, parcel office, signal box, platform and an L&SWR third-class coach. The latter is now a self-catering unit and the old waiting room can be hired for private functions.

Maps
Landranger 1:50,000 Sheet 185. Pathfinder 1:25,000 Sheet SU 23/ 33 Map Reference of Start/Finish SU345304

How to get there
From Winchester follow A272 west to Stockbridge. From Basingstoke go there via Sutton Scotney. In the village, turn at the first roundabout onto the A3057 towards Romsey. After 3 miles pass through King's Somborne, then bear off right onto a lane for Horsebridge. Hampshire Bus service 32 between Winchester and Salisbury via Stockbridge passes through Houghton and Broughton (Monday-Saturday). Alight at Houghton Corner or in the square at Broughton to start the walk instead of at Horsebridge. On Sundays service 901 passes through King's Somborne to Salisbury. Alight at the church

Left; A Columbarium or dovecote, rebuilt in 1684, stands in the churchyard.

(cont. from prev. page) and follow the Clarendon Way for half a mile to this walk.

Pub facilities
The John O'Gaunt is ideally situated on the Test Way and is already a popular destination for walkers who enjoy hearty portions of good home-cooked food available at this friendly and welcoming pub. The one bar is usually full with walkers, cyclists and locals alike on weekend lunchtimes, enjoying the three well-priced and well-kept real ales — Palmers IPA, Ringwood Forty-niner and King Alfred — and choosing food from the daily black-board menu, which may include a warming home-made soup, steak & kidney pudding, chicken and ham pie and a vegetarian quiche. Walking parties catered for with prior notice. Pub hours 1130-1430 (Saturday 1100-1500) and 1800-2300 with the normal Sunday hours. No food Tuesday evenings. Walkers can park in the large Test Way car park opposite.

The atmosphere of bygone steam days can be relived in this nostalgic scene.

On the opposite side of the valley is the long straggling village of Houghton. The oldest and most exclusive fishing club in the country is named after the village, founded in 1822 and limited to only 17 members. It has its headquarters in the Grosvenor Hotel in Stockbridge.

Further west along the Clarendon Way is the large and attractive village of Broughton situated on Wallop Brook. Wallop simply means 'valley of the stream' and this village of timbered houses and well-kept farmhouses surrounded by walls with thatched tops follows the course of the Wallop Brook for nearly a mile.

The church of St Mary is 12th and 13th century with short pillars and high-pointed arches, and boasts a beautiful stained glass window by Kempe from 1904. In 1314 the then Rector was given an endowment in the form of a 'Columbarium' or dovecote and its successor, rebuilt in 1684 stands in the churchyard. The circular, brick dovecote could house 482 pairs of pigeons and the young pigeons (squabs) provided an important source of protein all year round. The key to the dovecote can be obtained to view the interior, which was restored in 1984 to mark National Heritage Year.

Just south of Broughton is the route of the former Roman road which ran between Old Sarum, just outside the modern Salisbury, to Winchester. The old road leads back down into the Test valley to the hamlet of Bossington with its large mellow brick and gabled manor built in 1834. The tiny church belonging to the manor and situated in the meadows was locked on our visit, with no indication of where to obtain a key.

The Roman road crossed the River Test near Horsebridge and it is believed the Normans revived the old road, because it allowed easy access from the palace at Clarendon to a palace that probably existed in King's Somborne, a mile beyond Horsebridge. John of Gaunt, son of Edward III is said to have had a palace here in the 14th century, where he created a huge deer park for his hunting and which is still marked on present day maps and remembered in the name of the pub in Horsebridge.

The Greyhound
This Marston's pub at Broughton was originally an old coaching inn. Today it is popular for its food with a wide range of snacks, salads, grills and daily specials. It is open from 1130-1430 and 1900-2300, all day on Saturdays and the usual times on Sundays. It is the home of the famous Broughton Pumpkin Club. Walkers may use the car park if permission is asked.

The Tally Ho
This pub has been in the same family for over 100 years, the present landlord is over 90! It is a simple, old-fashioned, two-bar village local owned by Whitbread. No food is available and there are no facilities for children. A rarity indeed.

Walk 4.

Distance: *Allow four-and-a-half hours for this seven-and-half mile walk.*

From the Test Way car park opposite the John O'Gaunt turn right passing Horsebridge Mill on your right and cross the bridge over one of the many gently flowing channels that make up the River Test. At the green fingerpost ahead of you, waymarking the Test Way, turn right down onto the route of the old railway line. The pathway passes through a thicket area bordering the watermeadows away to your left. This is a good spot for Nightingales in May, when they are in full song as dusk begins to fall.

Beyond an old bridge, the path widens becoming a gravel track and now resembles an old railway route. When you reach a wooden gate turn left onto a trackway waymarked 'Clarendon Way', the long distance walk which links Salisbury and Winchester. This track takes you across the broad expanse of watermeadows and over three bridges which span the river channels of the Test. Pause for a while on the bridges, for the river scenes are truly peaceful. The sweet and clear waters of the Test are bordered by reeds and willows and swans often grace the picture, gliding effortlessly up or downstream and trout may be seen swimming in the shallows, the peace only broken by little more than the plop of a fish leaping or the swish of a fishing line.

After crossing the wooden footbridge, follow the track to a metal gate, pass through the gap on the left and turn left along the lane, you are now in the village of Houghton. Cross over and when you reach Lavender Cottage turn right to follow the Clarendon Way along a metalled lane. Go round the gate ahead of you onto an old cobbled track, which gradually ascends through arable land, taking you out of the Test valley. Shortly, after passing a barn on your left, the route becomes grassy and may be muddy after wet weather and regular use by farm vehicles. The track affords good views down into the picturesque and green valley created by Wallop Brook before you pass to the right of a small copse. Proceed gently downhill with the village of Broughton nestling in the valley to your left.

Pass through a gap in the hedge and drop down onto a track, turning right, then almost immediately left at the fingerpost, onto a grassy path to the rear of the houses in Broughton village. You now keep to the left-hand hedge into another field and climb the stile ahead of you. Shortly, bear left off the field (black arrow) onto a trackway beside a wall, which soon gives way to a path leading you in front of some large metal gates to a stile. Cross this, keep left along the field edge and turn left at the fingerpost ahead of you. Climb another stile and proceed along a narrow path between a fence and a hedge before you bear right onto a lane and cross Wallop Brook.

Walk towards the village centre until you reach a small metal gate on your left and enter St Mary's churchyard. The grassy path takes you to the right of the magnificent 17th century brick dovecote, then bears left along a tarmac path past the church entrance and out to a lane, opposite the Tally Ho pub. The Greyhound is visible to your right.

You are now in High Street, turn left until you reach West View Stores, where you turn right onto a signed path beside a high wall. Bear left at the end of the wall and climb the stile that flanks a gate, then keep to the right-hand edge of the field to another stile in the corner. Your route proceeds along a narrow pathway to the rear of gardens, shortly becoming grassy with open fields and Broughton Hill away to your right.

Cross a stile onto a gravel driveway and where this bears sharp left, keep ahead, then bear left onto a track and almost immediately turn right towards a metal gate. Bear left before the gate to follow a grassy pathway between a hedge and a wooden fence. We found this path to be quite

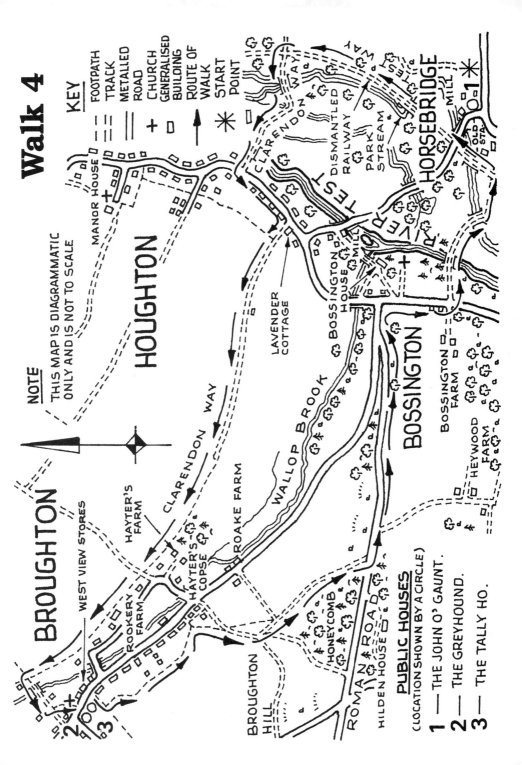

overgrown and it certainly looked little used. Persevere and climb a double stile, then another stile beyond the gap between fields and walk along a narrow defined path to where four footpaths converge. Go over the stile on your right, head straight across the field in front of you and cross the double stile in the fence to the right of the last bungalow. Proceed to the next stile visible ahead and drop down onto an old sunken lane.

You now turn right and gradually walk uphill to a junction of paths. Ignore the fingerpost pointing uphill, bear left along the green lane beside a hedge affording views down Wallop Brook into the Test valley. The grassy track soon gives way to a narrow pathway which takes you uphill through the edge of woodland. Halfway up, rest for a moment where a tree has fallen, to absorb the cameo view encapsulating rolling arable land, lush meadowland and distant views across to Stockbridge Down beyond the Test valley. Refreshed, proceed uphill through a mix of old coppice and beech woodland and bear left along a lane. You are now following the course of the Roman road. Remain on the lane for three-quarters of a mile down to a T-junction where you turn right and shortly, right again at the next T-junction ahead. Pass the little chapel in the meadow away to your left, which was locked when we tried the door.

Turn left onto a track opposite the last brick cottage on your right and follow this to the River Test. Cross two bridges, then climb the stile beside the gate in front of you and proceed half-right across meadowland to a stile in the hedge. At the time we walked across this meadow archaeologists were searching for remains of the Roman road which is thought to have crossed the River Test here. Beyond the stile you turn left onto the Test Way, passing the old railway station at Horsebridge which has been preserved more or less as it was when it closed in 1964. Cross an old railway bridge over the river and shortly turn right onto the lane back across the river to the John O'Gaunt.

Harewood Forest paths and tracks from Longparish

WALK 5
At least **3 hours**
6 miles
Walk begins page 30

Background to the walk

Longparish certainly lives up to its name for it is very long, stretching for three miles along the River Test and incorporating the hamlets of Forton, Middleton and East Aston. The village was originally known as Middleton, before its nickname 'Longparish' superseded it. It is a picturesque, rural community, comprising thatched cottages of brick, flint or timber-frame or a combination of all three and has in the recent past won the Best Kept Village Competition for Hampshire.

The church of St Nicholas is in the hamlet of Middleton and is mainly 13th century, although much restored in Victorian times. Of particular note is the handsome chequered stone and flint tower constructed in the 15th century and the set of stocks near the lych gate — a reproduction of the original — date from about 1930. Inside, there is an 18th century bird-bath type font and many memorials to the Hawker family.

Colonel Peter Hawker was a famous 19th century sportsman who lived at Longparish House and whose sporting diaries, published in 1893, included much detail about the shooting and fishing in the area. He recorded details of how much game and fish he had shot or caught and he reckoned to have caught around a ton of trout from the Test here.

On two occasions the walk crosses the former track of the Hurstbourne to Fullerton branch railway, which once connected with the London to Salisbury line. It was built in 1885 and was a

Maps
Landranger 1:50,000 Sheet 185. Pathfinder 1:25,000 Sheet SU 44/ 54 Map Reference of Start/Finish SU428440

How to get there
From Winchester follow the B3420 northwards to join the A34 to Bullington Cross, where you turn left onto the A303 towards Andover. After 3 miles turn right onto the B3048 signposted to Longparish. From Basingstoke take the A303 from the A30 (or M3) for Bullington Cross and Andover. The Plough lies on your left in the heart of Longparish, beyond the church. Parking is available at the pub, if permission is asked first or at the village hall near the church. Hampshire Bus service 30 and 31 (Sunday only) between Winchester and Andover passes through Longparish.

favourite with Queen Victoria, who asked for the royal trains to be routed along the line whenever she travelled to Southampton. Longparish station was situated beyond the A303 and is now a private house known as Smallwood Lodge. It was here in 1927 that scenes from the original film version of 'The Ghost Train' were filmed. Passenger trains ceased running in 1931, although freight trains used the line until 1956.

Much of the walk threads its way through parts of Harewood Forest, once a royal hunting ground and more recently used as an ammunition storage area during the Second World War. The concrete roads serving the depot can still be seen. Nowadays the forest is a peaceful place to explore, across a network of footpaths through mixed deciduous woodland. The area is haven to a diverse collection of wildlife, particularly noted for its moths, beetles and deer and for the carpets of Bluebells in spring.

Of all the footpaths that criss-cross Harewood Forest, the Test Way is the best-known and most walked. This long-distance walk traverses Hampshire for a distance of 48 miles between Totton at the seaward end and Inkpen Beacon in Berkshire. Twenty-seven miles of it follows the Test valley, the remainder following the line of the River Bourne. Much of our walk enjoys the well-defined tracks and paths of the Way, following the clearly marked green arrows and TW logo.

Walk 5.

Distance: *Allow at least three hours for this six-and-a-half mile walk.*

On leaving the Plough cross over the B3048, turn right and walk a little way to a gravel driveway beside St Nicholas school. Bear left here with the green arrow indicating the Test Way — which will accompany you on much of this walk — painted on an old lamp-post directing you towards the church lych gate. You now have the choice of

Pub facilities
The Plough
Popular for both its home cooked bar food and the interesting restaurant menu, which brings people from far and wide to this creeper covered village pub. Food is served daily between 1130-1430 and from 1900-2215. Pub hours are 1100-1500 and 1800-2300 on weekdays, the usual hours on Sunday. The pub is owned by Whitbread and four real ales are available includung Castle Eden Ale and Strongs Country. In the bar area, daily changing blackboard menus include a range of ploughmans and triple-decker sandwiches plus hot dishes such as hearty home-made pies — steak and kidney and chicken, bacon and mushroom served with fresh vegetables — and a range of fresh fish. Children are allowed in the pub if they are eating, but dogs are forbidden in the bar. However, on fine days the delightful garden is the place to be, in one of the secluded areas among the mature shrubs, flower borders and climbing roses.

either following the waymarked Test Way around the perimeter of the church, or you can walk through the churchyard to rejoin the Test Way beyond another gate. We chose the latter as the church door is always open, welcoming visitors to this attractive building set in meadowland.

The Test Way at this point crosses lush meadowland, linking the hamlet of Middleton to the picturesque group of houses known as Forton. The defined path takes you through two wooden gates before you bear left onto a tiny lane into Forton. Unfortunately, the peace and quiet of this quaint, typically Hampshire scene of thatched, brick and timber cottages is spoilt by the incessant roar of traffic on the nearby A303. At the sharp right-hand bend follow the road round, the Test Way bears off left continuing its journey down the river valley.

When you reach the T-junction with the B3048 at the boundary of Longparish, cross over and pass through a wooden gate onto a waymarked path that has been reinstated through a crop field. Shortly, you will join a gravel track, bear right and cross the course of the old Hurstbourne to Fullerton branch railway, remaining on the track between arable fields and a land infill site. Watch out for large lorries making their way to the site, making sure you are upwind of the clouds of dust that are thrown up.

Bear left when you reach a copse and scrubland, where the main track veers right, to follow a narrow path along the edge of a field to the left of the copse. You then turn right onto another farm track, only to turn immediately left onto a grass track which soon bears left-handed along a line of oak trees and along the base of a shallow valley. Where the track divides, proceed ahead with the mature tree-lined hedgerow to your left. When you reach a beech copse, bear left onto a more defined track, then keep right towards the green gates visible ahead and pass through the gap beside them onto a lane. Turn left and look for a gap in the hedge on your right and join a grass path between arable fields, which is waymarked by a broken, old-style fingerpost. The path keeps to the right of the wood ahead, its border was full of aromatic wild thyme when we walked this way.

Shortly, bear left away from the field following the grass path to the right

of some birch trees to the main trackway into Harewood Forest. We found the next stretch of the walk very peaceful, offering excellent opportunities to view the flora and fauna that abound throughout the woodland. We found the bridleway to be quite muddy underfoot in places, as it explores the mixed woodland of predominantly oak, hazel and birch. They are a haven to woodpeckers, finches and many songbirds and if you are lucky, as we were, deer can be seen in the bracken-covered clearings.

When you reach a crossroads of tracks at a large conifer tree keep straight on, the footpath sign waymarking your route is nailed to the tree. Eventually you will join a gravel track, which leads you to the busy B3400 Andover to Whitchurch road. Turn right along the road for a little way to an old pub — the cradle which once held the sign is still in place — and cross over the road to join a gravel, then tarmac lane which takes you through Andover Farm and its small industrial site. Pass through a metal gate where you will find beyond the wood pile on your right a charcoal burner. This was smoking away during its cooking stage as we passed.

At the black metal gates and driveway to a house, bear left onto the grass around the perimeter of its grounds and join a hedged bordered grass track and follow this downhill towards the farm complex visible ahead of you. When you do arrive at Faulkners Down Farm turn right onto a metalled lane and rejoin the Test Way, noting the green arrows on the fence to your

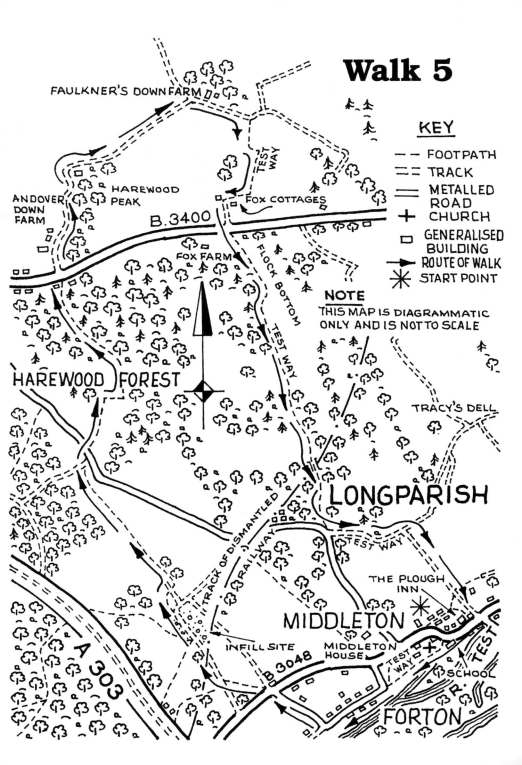

Longparish church, set in lush meadowland.

right. Proceed d o w n h i l l, turning right at the 'Private Road, no thoroughfare' sign onto a grass and gravel track between arable fields. Shortly, the green arrows direct you through a wide gap in the hedge, then around the left-hand edge of a large field. A group of deer were happily grazing in the far corner as we quietly made our way to the stile located near Fox Cottages. Climb this, bear left through a wooden gate and follow the tarmac driveway to the B3400.

Cross over the road and the stile beyond to follow the 'TW' painted logo and arrow, pointing you along a grass path bordered by crops. This soon develops into a wide grass track flanked on one side by rolling arable land. At this point we were pleasantly surprised to here the gentle 'mewing' call of a pair of buzzards as they soared over the woodland ahead. This is still a rare sight indeed these days across the Hampshire countryside, although a few pairs are known to breed in the county as their range has slowly spread eastwards from Dorset.

The grass track gradually climbs uphill, soon giving way to a stony track which passes beneath a fine beech tree canopy. Shortly, bear left onto a narrow woodland path which soon leads you out onto a gravel track, turn left here and follow the green arrows on the trees back over the old railway. Your arrowed route bears left downhill to a green Test Way fingerpost directing you right along a tree-lined track towards Longparish ahead. Proceed ahead on joining a metalled lane and disregard the green arrow on your right waymarking the Test Way in front of a row of cottages and continue down to the B-road in the village. Turn right along the road, taking care as it can be busy, back to the Plough.

Bourne Valley footpaths around St. Mary Bourne

WALK 6
Allow 2 $^1/_2$ hours
4 $^1/_2$ miles
Walk begins page 37

Background to the walk

St Mary Bourne, locally known as plain 'Bourne', nestles in the valley of the delightfully-named Bourne Rivulet, which rises at Hurstbourne Tarrant and idly flows through St Mary Bourne, joining the Test beyond Hurstbourne Priors. The rivulet is an intermittent tributary of the Test, in summer months it dries up, only to be reborn again in the spring after the winter rains soak the underlying chalk.

Downstream from the village near the huge nine-arch viaduct which carries the London to Salisbury railway, the Bourne has been utilised to feed a large area of watercress beds. These beds are owned by Hampshire Watercress and their product is marketed throughout the country as 'Vitacress'.

The centre of the village around the church and river bridge is very attractive. The main street is lined with old cottages, some thatched and timber-framed such as the Old Plough, formerly an inn and Hillview Cottages, perhaps the oldest in the village. Near the river bridge over the Bourne Rivulet there is a cast-iron street lamp, which was erected in 1897 to commemorate the diamond jubilee of Queen Victoria. It is the only surviving lamp-post — the rest were melted down in a scrap-metal drive during the Second World War — and was restored and wired for electricity to commemorate the present Queen's silver jubilee.

The church of St Peter dates from about 1157 and has an Elizabethan tower. Inside, the most

Maps

Landranger 1:50,000 Sheet 185. Pathfinder 1:25,000 Sheet SU 25/ 35 and SU 44/54 Map Reference of Start/ Finish SU422504

How to get there

From Winchester follow the B3420 north and join the A34 towards Newbury. At Bullington Cross turn left onto the A303 in the direction of Andover and after 3 miles turn right onto the B3048. Pass through Longparish to Hurstbourne Priors where you cross the B3400 to follow the Bourne valley for 2 miles to St Mary Bourne. From Basingstoke follow the B3400 out to Whitchurch and turn right at Hurstbourne Priors. Hampshire Bus service 31 between Winchester and Newbury via Andover stops at the school in St Mary Bourne (Monday to Saturday only).

Pub facilities
The George

This old coaching inn enjoys a prime position in the attractive heart of the village, being located opposite the small bridge over the Bourne. The chequered effect brickwork exterior hides a traditional, unadorned village local, part of which used to be the butcher's shop before the last war. A warm welcome awaits visitors to this simply furnished free house, which is becoming very popular for its value-for-money bar food. The menu is chalked up on the blackboard and may include chilli, steak and kidney pie, sweet and sour pork, lamb cutlets, chicken and mushroom pie, fish and chips and an 8oz. steak, the price of which includes a pint or a glass of wine! A full roast or a range of ploughmans is available on Sunday lunch-times. To quench your thirst their are two real ales, well conditioned Wadworth 6X and Tetley Bitter. Being situated on the Test Way it is regularly frequented by walkers and groups of walkers are welcomed and well- catered for if

important object is the Norman Tournai marble font, the largest of four Tournai black marble fonts that exist in the county, one of the others being in Winchester cathedral. This one is particularly fine, with its attractive carving of doves drinking out of cups, a quite rare example of Norman decoration. Also of note is the original 17th century reading desk with four positions for the Bible. One of the chains which formerly secured the Bible to the table is still in place

A fair-cum-carnival was held annually until 1830 in the Summerhaugh — the open space in

*Right : Village scene in
St Mary Bourne*

advance notice is
given. Food is served
daily from 1200-1400
and 1900-2200. Pub
hours are 1100-1430
and 1800-2300, with
the usual Sunday
hours. Dogs are al-
lowed in the bars and
children can use the
separate games room.

the centre of the village — and was known as the 'Bourne Revel'. The
festival certainly lived up to its name with such events as 'cudgelling' or
'backswording' held on a platform built over the river. Young men known
as backsworders struck each other on the head with cudgells — extra
marks were awarded if the blood ran down further than an inch. 'Jingling'
was another activity, a variation on the theme of 'Blind Mans Bluff', in
which the jingler — a man carrying bells — had to be caught by his
blindfolded opponents. The prize was generally a cheese or a barrel of beer
for the jingler who evaded capture, but the man who caught him could
claim a purse of money.

In the past it was said locally that 'those born in the village would live
as long as they liked'. A list drawn up from the Burials book between 1826
and 1883 gave the names of 16 people who lived to over 90. St Mary Bourne
is certainly a most peaceful, rural place in which to live to a great age.

Walk 6.

Distance: *Allow two-and-a-half hours for this four-and-a-half mile walk.*

As the car park of The George is small and the pub busy at most times,
it is best to park your car at the recreation area car park which is situated
across the bridge from the George and along the first lane on your left.

Leave the car park at the broken fingerpost — it had no finger when we
passed it — in the left-hand corner, near the entrance and bear half-right
skirting the cricket pitch towards a telegraph pole, situated to the left of
the wooden pavilion ahead of you. Climb the stile in the hedgerow, your
route being waymarked by the Test Way green arrow and proceed across
a pasture on a defined path to another stile and a lane. Cross over the lane

and the stile flanking the brick wall to your right, then keep to the right-hand edge of an arable field to another stile.

Climb the stile and bear diagonally right with the green arrow across a meadow towards a house. You now pass through a small wooden gate where a Test Way sign keeps you on course, as you turn left along a metalled lane passing the driveway to 'Haven Hill'. Keep left as the lane gives way to a stony track and turn right at the stile and fingerpost directly ahead of you. A fenced pathway keeps you to the left of a bungalow to another stile, beyond which you walk along the right-hand edge of the field to a stile beside a metal gate and to the rear of some houses which lie to your right. Shortly, bear left uphill on a well-worn path across pasture to a stile visible in the hedgerow in front of you.

Here you bear right into a small copse, then you keep to the edge of a field which affords beautiful views across the rural Bourne valley. After crossing the stile ahead, you bear right onto a lane, then immediately left at the Test Way fingerpost through a gap in the hedge. Your path gradually ascends, keeping close to the hedge on your right. Eventually, the green arrow directs you through a wide field entrance where you now follow the tree-lined hedge left-handed uphill.

Pause for a moment on reaching the next stile to savour the panoramic

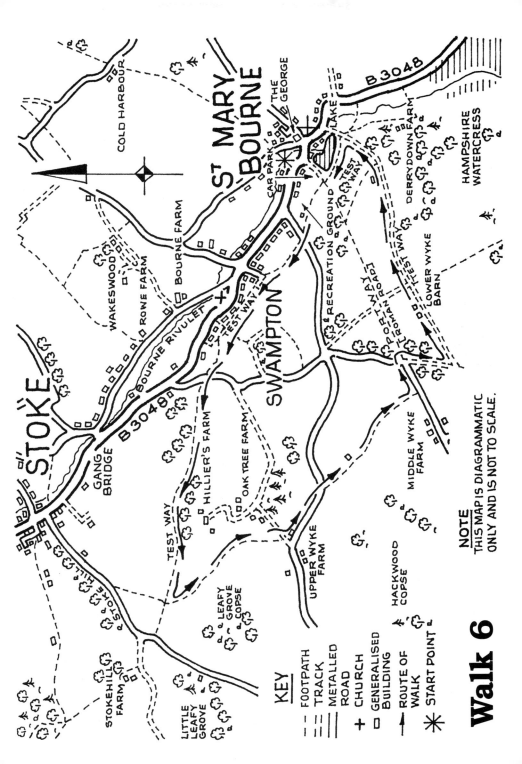

Walk 6

KEY

-- -- FOOTPATH
= = TRACK
—— METALLED ROAD
✝ CHURCH
◻ GENERALISED BUILDING
→ ROUTE OF WALK
✳ START POINT

NOTE
THIS MAP IS DIAGRAMMATIC ONLY AND IS NOT TO SCALE.

S^T MARY BOURNE

STOKE

SWAMPTON

COLD HARBOUR

THE GEORGE

B 3048

HAMPSHIRE WATERCRESS

DERRYDOWN FARM

LAKE

CAR PARK

TEST WAY

RECREATION GROUND

LOWER WYKE BARN

PORT WAY (ROMAN ROAD)

TEST WAY

BOURNE FARM

WAKESWOOD

ROWE FARM

BOURNE RIVULET

TEST WAY

HILLIER'S FARM

OAK TREE FARM

UPPER WYKE FARM

MIDDLE WYKE FARM

GANG BRIDGE

B 3048

STOKE HILL

STOKEHILL FARM

LITTLE LEAFY GROVE

LEAFY GROVE COPSE

HACKWOOD COPSE

views that are beginning to unfold across the Hampshire 'highlands', an area of rolling downland that stretches from beyond Inkpen Beacon to Basingstoke. From here, your route keeps to the left-hand hedge, crossing three stiles and as many pastures. Just beyond the third stile, climb a stile in the hedge on your left and once in the field beyond, bear half-left towards the far left-hand corner to cross a stile in the bramble-covered wire fence.

Turn left and follow the fence to what we found to be a broken-stepped stile in the corner. With views to your left back down into the Bourne valley, bear half-right across a large open pasture, keeping to the right of the houses visible ahead. On reaching the corner of the field, turn right onto a stony track and pass in front of two houses on your right before turning left at the telephone box onto a narrow lane.

Remain on the lane with a copse to your right to where it bears round a left-hand bend. Here you veer right through a wide gap beside an oak tree into an arable field and keep left along an overgrown grass track that flanks a wire fence. Pass in front of a small building and enjoy the open vistas — west towards Andover and beyond to the rolling landscape that signifies the edge of Salisbury Plain.

At the end of the field, proceed ahead where your grass track passes between a fence and a tree-lined hedge down to a narrow lane and turn left. You are now on the route of an old Roman road, known as The Portway, which once linked Silchester to Old Sarum. It was here, to the west of St Mary Bourne in 1879, that a stretch of Roman paving was destroyed because it interfered with farming practices. How little were historical sites valued then!

On reaching a sharp left-hand bend you turn right along a waymarked grass path and pass to the side of a red metal gate, then between mature tall hedges. Shortly, bear left at a junction of tracks and rejoin the Test Way long distance walk which at this point follows an old hedge-bordered green lane. Where this track bears left proceed ahead along a signed, grass centred stony track to a metalled lane and follow this downhill into the tranquil Bourne valley.

As you enter St Mary Bourne, turn left just before the first house on your left at the Test Way fingerpost which notifies you that Inkpen Beacon is 11 miles away. This established path takes you along the base of the hill with a large lake to your right. This was created a few years ago by the local doctor. Pass through a small wooden gate onto the recreation ground and turn right along the edge of the cricket ground back to your transport.

Border paths and tracks around Tangley

Background to the walk

There is no real centre to the village of Tangley, houses are spread along the numerous tree-lined lanes that criss-cross this well-wooded and hilly parish. The church of St Thomas enjoys a peaceful spot, isolated from the main clusters of cottages and surrounded by trees at the edge of Fox plantation. It was built in 1875 by William White, who created an unusual feature by inserting lines of tiles within the church walls. It is certainly worth taking the time to knock on the door of Church View cottage next door to obtain the church key. Inside is the only lead font in Hampshire and one of only thirty similar fonts that survive throughout England. Decorated with thistles and roses, it dates from the early 17th century. Lead fonts used to be a common sight in churches across the country, but unfortunately many have been melted down over the years, a practice that was particularly prevalent during the war years.

Also located within the parish of Tangley is the spread-out village of Hatherden. Picturesque thatched cottages and Victorian estate cottages are interspersed with modern dwellings, many of them lining the parkland of Hatherden House. One particular building of interest in the village is the school, the oldest part of which is a delightful two-storeyed brick building built in 1725. The school, opened in 1727, was originally provided for the education of 24 poor children and today is one of the oldest schools still in use in Hampshire.

Maps
Landranger 1:50,000 Sheet 185. Pathfinder 1:25,000 Sheet SU 25/ 35. Map reference of Start/Finish SU 334518.

How to get there
From Winchester head north on the B3420 to join the A34 towards Newbury. At Bullington Cross turn left onto the A303 for Andover. From Basingstoke leave the M3 at Exit 8 onto the A303 to Bullington Cross. After five miles leave the A303 to follow the A3093 signed to Andover and keep to the Ring Road and A303 signs. Encounter four roundabouts before joining the A349 Ring Road, also signed to Charlton. Leave the fifth roundabout for Charlton, passing through the village and keeping left at the next roundabout for Hatherden and Tangley. This lane

leads you to both The Hamster and The Fox.

Pub facilities
The Fox Inn
(pictured right) enjoys an isolated position on a fork of tiny lanes with rural views. The white-painted, brick and flint cottage-style building is over 300 years old and has been dispensing ales since 1830. The rustic, homely bars, complete with warming fires and the tiny restaurant are generally very busy with people seeking out the excellent home-cooked meals on offer, for The Fox has a reputation for its fine food for miles around. Walkers are welcomed, as are children and well-behaved dogs on leads. Choose from a hearty range of good value dishes chalked up on two daily-changing blackboard menus, one for lunch and the other for dinner. Lunch meals include ploughmans, salads, pies, good curries and a range of fresh pasta dishes with more imaginative dishes available in the evening. The bar is open from 1100-1500 and 1800-2300 on weekdays (usual times on Sundays). Three

Over a mile of our walk follows the course of an old Roman road, between Tangley and Hatherden. It is known in this area as 'The Chute Causeway' and was once an important thoroughfare from the Channel ports via Winchester to Cirencester, one of the largest Roman towns in the country. Much of it is now metalled in this part of Hampshire and Wiltshire, except for the delightful tree-lined track which we follow on this walk.

Walk 7.

Distance: *a little under eight miles, allow between four and five hours for leisurely walking.*

Leaving the Fox turn left along the narrow lane which gradually ascends through overhanging trees. Just beyond Bramble Cottage on your left, a footpath fingerpost directs you into mixed woodland. Follow the narrow path uphill through Fox Plantation which soon gives way to a grass and gravel track leading to the delightful church of St Thomas at Tangley. Set as it is in a splendid isolated position, surrounded by yew trees it is well worth a visit. You can obtain the key from Church View Cottage next door.

Your route from the church bears right onto the lane beyond the flagpole on the tiny green, which you follow downhill beneath a fine canopy of trees. Pass a lane off to your right, then bear right onto a stony track beyond Chalkpit Cottages and keep to the left of the thatched cottage in front of you. You are now on the course of an old Roman road, known as Chute Causeway. The wide trackway is a mix of cobble and gravel, often retaining pockets of muddy water after wet weather and as you would expect it is very straight, flanked on either side by mature tree-lined hedgerows. In places, where the hedge thins, you can enjoy cameo views south across arable land towards Andover.

After approximately a mile the old Roman road reaches a crossroads of metalled lanes. Here you turn right with Hatherden Park and House in the trees to your left, following the lane into the village of Hatherden. Bear left when you reach the road junction opposite Christ Church onto what can be a busy country thoroughfare. In a short distance the thatched roof of the Hamster comes into view.

For those of you not wishing to visit the pub, turn right at the green footpath fingerpost, located beyond a couple of brick and flint cottages. The narrow, fenced path passes between two dwellings to a stile. Climb the stile into a pasture and bear half-right to a gap visible in the hedgerow. Here you turn left through a further gap into the next field, before turning immediately right across the pasture to a stile flanking a metal gate in the hedgerow. Cross the narrow lane beyond the stile to another stile, where the yellow arrow markers direct you right-handed along the hedge.

Your route now takes you across two stiles located in the corners of as many fields, then along the right-hand edge of an arable field, passing a farmhouse to your right. Cross a gravel farm track onto a clearly visible path across a large crop field to the edge of woodland. Keep ahead with the wood to your left, turning left when you reach a narrow, hedged lane. Beyond a farmyard and a brick and flint cottage on your left, veer off right onto a waymarked footpath along a grass track.

well-conditioned real ales are served on handpumps and there is an excellent wine list. Food is available from 1200-1400 and 1830-2200. Walkers welcome to use car park if permission is asked first.

Also in Tangley is **The Cricketers**, *(featured on the cover of this book) an old drovers pub built around 1770. It was the last stopping place for sheep drovers taking their flocks to Weyhill Fair, five miles to the south. Tucked between two large estates — Tangley and Chute — it is a regular place for the local hunt and shooting parties to meet and features a wide range of game on its menu. You can enjoy wild boar, venison, pigeon or partridge amongst other game in season as well as fresh fish, grills, hearty pies, casseroles and curries and a choice of four different roasts on Sundays. Eat in the unspoilt drovers bar with its huge inglenook or in the comfortable dining area to the rear and quench your thirst with one of the eight real ales on offer. Food* can be ordered from 1200-1400 and 1900-2130 except on Sunday evenings, the bar being open from 1100-1500 and 1800-2300. Children are welcome as are dogs and you may park in the car park if you ask first.

The Hamster
(pictured right) in Hatherden is an attractive thatched 16th century cottage which has been extended and made open-plan inside. It is a free house serving a range of real ales including Ringwood and Gibbs Mew brews which are served from 1200-1500 and 1900-2300, except Monday lunchtimes when the pub is closed. An extensive bar menu includes sandwiches, jacket potatoes, fresh fish, grills, chilli and a good selection of vegetarian dishes. On our visit the specials were a choice of five curries. There is also a restaurant. Food is served from 1200-1400 and 1900-2200. Children well-catered for with their own menu and a play area in the garden. Ask first to park here for your walk, there should be no problem.

On reaching a wire fence across your path you are diverted right into a field, where you follow the left-hand edge along the line of the telegraph wire to the second pole located in the far corner. Turn left along a grass track which keeps to the right of a line of oak trees, downhill to a crossroads of lanes beside a disused chapel. Turn right here, then cross over the main lane into a T-road which lies to the right of a group of houses known as St Margarets. Gradually walk uphill, along the lane in front of the houses to where it bears right. Here you fork left along a hedged trackway, which leads you downhill to a T-junction of tracks where you turn right, the track soon giving way to a bridleway through the edge of woodland. When you reach a track that veers left uphill, keep ahead remaining on the bridleway, now narrow and hedged, following the valley bottom.

You will soon enter a small copse where you pass an old dwelling to your left. Disregard the pathway on your right to pass through two metal gates and follow the narrow beech and hazel-lined path ahead of you. Beyond the trees at a gate, a yellow footpath arrow directs you along a defined grass path through the valley, known as Soper's Bottom. Your route keeps to the right of a solitary tree and proceeds to the small metal gate that flanks the woodland to your right. Ahead of you a

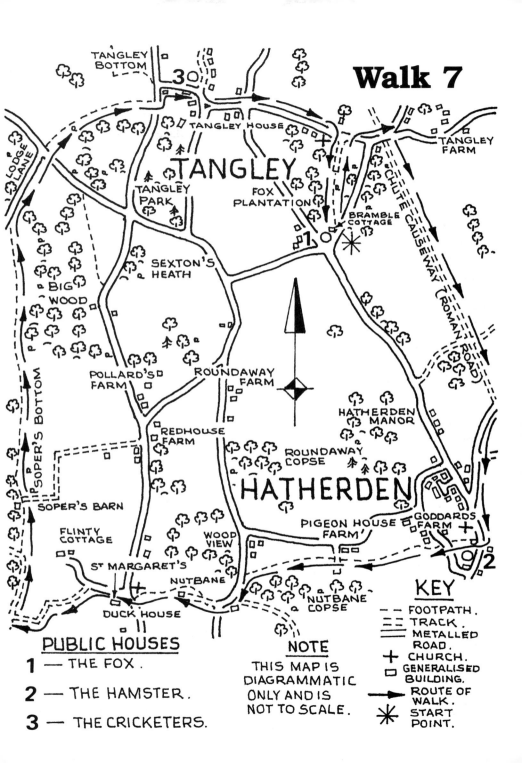

Walk 7

PUBLIC HOUSES

1 — THE FOX.

2 — THE HAMSTER.

3 — THE CRICKETERS.

NOTE

THIS MAP IS DIAGRAMMATIC ONLY AND IS NOT TO SCALE.

KEY

- - - FOOTPATH.
═ ═ TRACK.
═══ METALLED ROAD.
+ CHURCH.
□ GENERALISED BUILDING.
→ ROUTE OF WALK.
✳ START POINT.

St Thomas of Canterbury church at Tangley.

metal gate precedes a lush valley bottom pasture, which you cross to a wooden gate, before turning right for a little way along a muddy track to a lane. Bear right here to follow the tree canopied lane uphill to a T-junction.

A green fingerpost waymarks your route across the lane and along the left-hand edge of a field to a gap in the hedge. Here you can bear right onto a 'permissive path' around the field edge when the field is in crop — the official yellow arrowed path cuts across the field at other times. A further arrow, nailed to a tree, directs you down the field's left-hand edge to a stile and a lane. Walk left along the lane for a short distance with Tangley Park to your right, before turning right beyond a cottage to follow another lane into the village of Tangley. The Cricketers pub lies back from the lane to your left as you follow the lane right, then left at the next junction, downhill to a crossroads. Here you cross over, remaining on the lane to Tangley church, where you turn right to rejoin the outward footpath through Fox Plantation back to the Fox and your car.

Exploring old border tracks and paths from Vernham Dean

WALK 8
Allow **3 hours**
5 miles
Walk begins page 49

Background to the walk

The isolated, mainly thatched village of Vernham Dean lies in a valley high up in northern Hampshire, close to the Wiltshire and Berkshire borders. The parish name is Vernhams Dean and incorporates the hamlets of Vernham Street and Littledown to the north. Vernham was formerly called 'Ferneham' which means the 'village or meadow among ferns'.

The little church of St Mary is situated between Dean and Street and can be reached by following the lane beside The George, northwards. It mainly dates from 1851, having been rebuilt after a fire, although it does retain the original decorated Norman door. During the time when it was being rebuilt, services were held at Maceys Cottage nearby. Evidence of this can be seen in the odd appearance of the cottage. Gothic-style windows give it a chapel-like form from one side, while from the other it looks like a normal cottage. Just along the lane from the church is Vernham Manor, a fine example of a Jacobean brick house.

The plague or 'Black Death' that swept the country during the reign of Charles II had a profound effect on north Hampshire. This is reflected in the number of churches that are isolated from the main centres of habitation. Once the awful disease had struck a village, survivors quickly moved away from the affected area to re-establish the community a little further away on 'clean' land. Vernham Dean is one such village and a legend associated with the days of the

Maps
Landranger 1:50,000 Sheet 174. Pathfinder 1:25,000 Sheet SU 25/35. Map Reference of Start/Finish SU 341565.

How to get there
From Basingstoke take the A303 off the M3 for Bullington Cross. From Winchester head north via B3420 and join A34 to Newbury. At Bullington Cross bear left onto A303 for Andover, then after 5 miles you join A3093 signed Andover. Follow the 'Ring Road' signs across two roundabouts, then at the third take the third exit to join A343 towards Newbury. When you reach Hurstbourne Tarrant bear left onto a lane beyond the George and Dragon pub. Pass through Ibthorpe and Upton, remaining on the lane signed to Vernham Dean. The George Inn lies to your

right in the village
centre. It is possible to
park in the pub's car
park at the front of the
building, if permission
is asked first or in the
village hall car park
close by.

Pub facilities
The George Inn
(pictured right)
The 17th century
ground floor of The
George Inn is built of
alternate courses of
brick and flint sup-
ported by weathered
timbers, while the tiled
roof undulates grace-
fully above the win-
dows of the later, brick
upper storey. Inside
this attractive and
unspoilt country pub,
everything is spick and
span throughout the
three, heavily beamed,
inter-connected bars,
which are furnished
with a mix of comfort-
able chairs and sturdy
mahogany and oak
tables. Hearty, home-
cooked bar food, ideal
for walking appetites is
served daily from
1200-1400 and 1900-
2100. The short
blackboard menu may
offer large toasted
sandwiches, a warm-
ing soup such as leek
and potato, corned-beef
hash, cauliflower
cheese, rabbit stew, a
range of ploughmans

plague is still a topic of conversation around these
parts.

The story is that the Rector of the parish was in
fear of contracting the disease when it fell upon
the village, so he persuaded his parishioners who
had fallen victims to it to gather on Vernham Hill.
Informing them he was going to Andover to bring
them supplies, he fled in selfish terror, leaving
them to starve. While still on Vernham Hill justice
overtook him and he fell victim to the infection and
died. Since then his ghost is said to haunt the
area. Many over the years have seen the grief
stricken figure wending his way up the hill. In
1949 a woman cycling to Fosbury reported seeing
a figure 'white from the waist upwards, wearing a
robe which swung from the movement of his legs'.
So if you are finishing this walk at dusk, look out
for this ghostly figure as you descend Knolls
Down, for your tale will certainly be of interest
once you reach the homely confines of The George.
An unusual sight in the village and passed towards
the end of our walk is the Methodist Chapel. It is
built right in front of Cheyney Cottage, an attractive
thatched 17th century cottage and almost com-
pletely obscures its view. Certainly a classic example of how poor planning regulations once were
in the mid-19th century.

as well as sweets like treacle tart. Marstons Best and Pedigree are the real ales available. On summer days the place to be is in the sheltered, flower-bordered garden to the rear. The bar is open from 1100-1430 (1500 on Saturdays) and 1800-2300 with the usual Sunday hours.

Walk 8.

Distance: *Allow three hours for this walk of 5 miles.*

Taking your leave from The George follow the main village street right-handed, shortly passing the telephone box and the Post Office. Just beyond the white thatched cottage where 'David' lives — the cottage is simply named David's Cottage — a footpath fingerpost directs you left along a grass centred stony track, beside a modern house. In a little way climb a stile that flanks a metal gate and remain on the track which gently rises uphill with views opening out to your right.

Your route soon veers right at a fork, the grassy track leading you towards woodland. Bracken and nettles may line the thick hedges as you enter the oak and hazel wood, your path maintaining its uphill route through the woodland edge. When we reached this spot, damp woodland aromas filled the air as the early morning sunlight flickered through the tree canopy, warming the dew-covered woodland foliage. At certain times of the year you will be dodging the wet and muddy patches, that linger beneath the dense canopy as you make your way along the track.

Disregarding the track that veers off to your right, keep ahead, the woodland will soon begin to thin. Emerge from the wood into an open pasture. Here a footpath sign points you uphill still, along a defined path passing a water trough to your left. Take a breather as you begin to crest the top of the hill, for behind you superb views have unfolded. Vernham Dean nestles in the valley and beyond, hedged fields and isolated farmsteads fill the undulating panorama towards Combe and Inkpen Beacon.

Your path soon passes through a young tree plantation to where a yellow arrow on a post, directs you into a small copse, to a stile. You are now on top of Conholt Hill which enjoys stunning views into Conholt Bottom, a dry valley that leads to Hippenscombe farm complex, visible in the distance. High above the combe is Knolls Down with Fosbury Hill Fort commanding the top. Beyond the stile, you follow the edge of the pasture left-handed along the mature hedgerow to another stile and a single-track lane. Your route takes you right, then at the grassy triangle and lane junction bear right again, to follow the lane down Conholt Hill.

In a short distance, just beyond a small parking area, climb a stile on your left and begin to descend half-left across the hillside, through scrub-covered grassland. The path is ill-defined, due to the hillside being criss-crossed with sheep tracks. You should head for the left-hand corner of the field, where the hedge joins the lane at the base of the hill. We had to

negotiate a low elec-
tric fence as we neared
the bottom, but we
believed it to be a very
temporary measure,
to keep the animals
from grazing the high
pastures.

Once over the stile
at the hedge, your
route bears west-
wards along the
metalled lane towards
the group of buildings
known locally as
Hippenscombe. This
valley bottom thoroughfare is little used by traffic and is a pleasurable part
of the walk. We were lucky enough to observe a pair of buzzards being
mobbed by angry crows, as they soared high above Fosbury Hill Fort to our
right. Eventually pass through a pair of wooden gates and enter
Hippenscombe. In a short way turn northwards along a concrete farm
road, towards a group of black barns.

It was here that we met one of the estate workers, who revealed to us that
Hippenscombe was once a much larger, thriving community, with a
notable 'William and Mary' style manor house (now demolished) dominating the hamlet. He also told us that the buzzards we had seen earlier
had bred in the woods, high up on Knolls Down. As we were about to leave,
to our surprise three lamas came over to the fence, an unusual sight
outside a zoo. Your route continues through the barn complex, bearing
right then left, before veering off right at a diesel tank onto a grass-cum-
earth track. This shortly gives way to an old green lane, bordered with elder
and hawthorn, as it gradually climbs the hillside affording views away to
your left across a quite unspoilt and remote landscape.

At the top of the hill the green lane meets a crossroads of ancient
routeways, which followed the highest points between settlements. Here
you turn eastwards, passing through a metal gate to join a fine old lane of
grass and loose stones. Undulating north Hampshire and Berkshire
countryside can be viewed from this high vantage point. The track soon
leads you to Fosbury Farm, where you cross its tarmac approach road,
maintaining your course eastwards along an established trackway. Keep
right at a fork in the track, your route passing between what was a nettle
covered bank and woodland before you enter a conifer and mixed deciduous woodland. Devoid of the sound of traffic, this peaceful stretch of

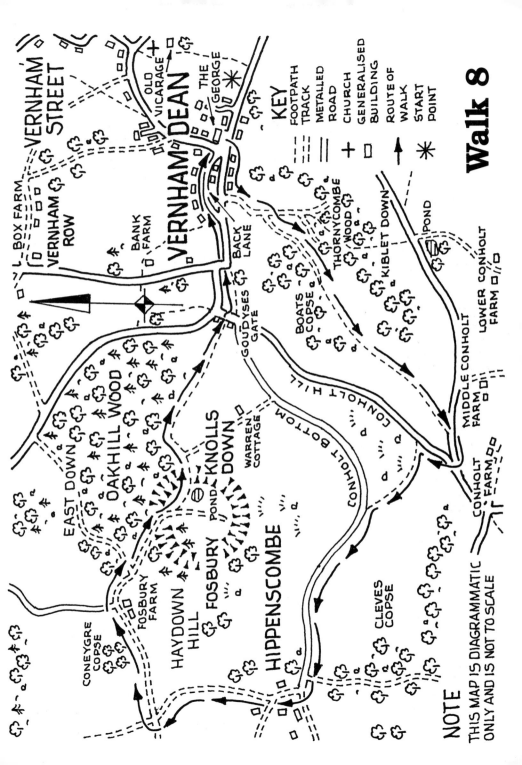

Walk 8

KEY

FOOTPATH — — — —
TRACK = = = =
METALLED ROAD
CHURCH +
GENERALISED BUILDING ▢
ROUTE OF WALK ↑
START POINT ✳

VERNHAM STREET

BOX FARM

VERNHAM ROW

BANK FARM

OLD VICARAGE

THE GEORGE

VERNHAM DEAN

BACK LANE

GOUDYSES GATE

THORNYCOMBE WOOD

BOATS COPSE

KIBLET DOWN

POND

LOWER CONHOLT FARM

MIDDLE CONHOLT FARM

CONHOLT HILL

CONHOLT BOTTOM

CONHOLT FARM

WARREN COTTAGE

KNOLLS DOWN

POND

OAKHILL WOOD

EAST DOWN

CONEYGRE COPSE

FOSBURY FARM

HAYDOWN HILL

FOSBURY

HIPPENSCOMBE

CLEVES COPSE

NOTE

THIS MAP IS DIAGRAMMATIC ONLY AND IS NOT TO SCALE

Oakhill Wood contained abundant birdlife.

When you reach a wide grassy avenue through the trees, bear right and pass through the gap in the beech-lined, raised earth wall, of the ancient Iron Age Hill Fort. Cross a stile and begin to head across Knolls Down, the lush pasture area that the fort encloses. In a short distance veer left along the lower path and pass to the left of a water-filled depression to a grass track, which takes you back through the fort embankment. With far-reaching views in front of you, follow the track downhill, parallel with the wood on your left. Climb the stile beside a metal gate and pass through a small copse into a huge arable field. Here you can look down along the main street in Vernham Dean, prior to following the field edge left-handed along a flint-strewn path, that leads you downhill to a drive between brick and flint cottages and a house. The house on your right was once a pub, the recess where its sign once fitted to the wall is still visible. On joining a lane you turn right, then in a little way bear left-handed at a fingerpost, which waymarks your route across a stile into a pasture. Here you follow the hedge right-handed to another stile, beyond which you keep right along the lane back into Vernham Dean. Bear left along Back Lane, to pass a fine selection of thatched properties and the Methodist Chapel before joining the main street and the welcoming sight of The George.

Through the Hampshire 'highlands' from Ashmansworth

WALK 9

At least **3 hours**

5 $^1/_2$ miles

Walk begins page 55

Background to the walk

The village of Ashmansworth extends for more than a mile along the chalk ridge of Hampshire's northern downland. It is the highest medieval village on chalk in England; at the Plough public house you are 770 feet above sea level and it is said to be about 3° Fahrenheit cooler. A very rural atmosphere pervades throughout the well-spaced mix of thatched and brick and flint cottages.

The beautiful old church of St James lies to the south and is quite unique, for it remains unrestored, escaping the severe Victorian restoration and alteration that was inflicted on many of Hampshire's churches. It is due to this that the church is noted for its medieval wall paintings of the 12th and 13th century. Unfortunately, they are very difficult to decipher. Gerald Finzi, the composer, lived in the village from 1937 and was best known for his music set to poetry. He died in 1956 and is buried beside the church porch. His tombstone was engraved by the artist Reynolds Stone and the memorial glass window in the porch is dedicated to English music. It depicts a tree with the initials of fifty English composers forming its roots.

The highest point in Hampshire, Pilot Hill at 937 feet, is just two miles away, close to the Berkshire/Hampshire border. Our walk incorporates Pilot Hill and the stunning views it affords across the Berkshire Vale. An old ox drove follows the crest of the ridge and was once used to drive sheep and cattle to and from markets in south-

Maps
Landranger 1:50,000 Sheet 174. Pathfinder 1:25,000 Sheets SU 45/55 and SU 25/35. Map Reference of Start/Finish SU 415575.

How to get there
From Basingstoke take A303 from M3 to Bullington Cross. From Winchester head north on B3420 to join A34 towards Newbury. When you reach Bullington Cross head westwards on A303 for Andover. After 5 miles along A303 turn left signed Andover, joining A3093, then keep ahead at the next two roundabouts following 'Ring Road' signs. At the third roundabout you take the third exit for Newbury, joining A343. Pass through Hurstbourne Tarrant before a sign directs you left towards Ashmansworth. There is generally plenty of room to park along the

main street near The Plough.

Pub facilities
The Plough

This rustic 'local' is over 200 years old. For the first century it was a simple alehouse and small-holding before becoming solely a pub. It is simply furnished, with a friendly atmosphere and dispenses real ale straight from the barrel — Archers Village Bitter, Golden and a stronger guest ale such as Fullers ESB. Hearty bar food is served lunchtimes only between 1200-1345, the blackboard menu offering soup, beef in beer, omelettes, ploughmans, home-made burgers with usually a fruit pie for pudding. Children have their own play area in an outbuilding, known as 'The Den'. Small garden to the side of the pub. The Plough is open from 1200-1430 and from 1800-2300 except for Monday lunchtime, also Tuesday lunchtimes between New Year and Easter.

The Jack Russell

in the estate village of Faccombe enjoys a peaceful spot opposite the pond. The pub dates from 1983, the

The Plough at Ashmansworth — a Free House.

east England. The long distance walk — The Wayfarers Walk — begins its traverse of Hampshire along this ancient route.

Faccombe is the most northerly village in the county and it is said to be of purely British derivation, no Roman remains having been found. The village was once known as Faccombe Upstreet, so named to distinguish it from Faccombe Netherton — now simply Netherton — a mile to the west. The latter was at one time the main centre of population, once having a 13th century church. It is only in the last 150 years that the bulk of the population has moved up the hill to Faccombe, where the church of St Barnabas was rebuilt in 1886 to serve the village. Little is left of Netherton, except for a couple of houses, an ex-rectory and a huge thatched barn.

Faccombe is centred around the large Georgian manor, with the majority of the houses, including the pub being owned by the estate. St Barnabas church commands a truly peaceful spot within the village and contains the decorated Norman font that once graced the original church in Netherton.

Walk 9.

Distance: *Allow at least three hours for this five-and-a-half mile walk.*

Your walk begins by turning right along the main village street away from The Plough, passing thatched cottages and Flint Cottage to the village green and war memorial. Here you bear right, the signpost directing you towards Faccombe. Pass Mere Cottage and follow the hedged lane downhill, with rolling downland views beginning to appear to your right. Disregard the yellow arrowed path on your left, remaining on the lane around the sharp right-hand bend ahead.

Immediately to your right, a fingerpost and stile flanking metal gates points your way across an arable field on a visible path towards the edge of the copse in front of you. A yellow arrow painted on a post directs you straight on, along the tree edge on a wide grassy path that drops sharply downhill. Beyond the copse, the defined pathway passes between two crop fields into the combe, to a track that precedes a woodland. A footpath sign directs you into what at first looks like an inaccessible copse, but after closer inspection a narrow nettled path threads its way up through the mixed copse. When you emerge from its overgrown confines bear right, then left across an unusual stepped stile that straddles an electric fence. Head half-left uphill across a pasture, keeping to the right of a clump of trees towards another stepped stile visible ahead.

North Hampshire must be one of the few places in the county that you can pause and enjoy the peace and quiet that surrounds you, without being rudely interrupted by the noise of car engines. Rural tranquility greets the eye here, sheep dot the pastures, the cotton reels of hay, fresh from harvesting, line the fields and the mewing of a lone Buzzard fills the early morning air as it soars above the wooded hill tops. We reluctantly left this peaceful sojurn, keeping left beyond the stile, onto a defined track through a young plantation into a wood, where the route was waymarked on a tree. A muddy track leads you through the quite dense, mixed

previous building — The George & Dragon — being demolished in 1980, before it fell down I was told. The pub has developed a popular food trade, the interesting dishes from the menu chalked up on blackboards, and served in the comfortable and sunny conservatory or in the carpeted bar. Main dishes include steak & kidney pie, chicken in tarragon sauce, chilli, chicken Madras, liver and bacon and a range of steaks and grills as well as sandwiches and ploughmans. Children have their own menu and are only allowed in the conservatory area. There is always a choice of two roasts for Sunday lunch. Food is served daily between 1200-1400 and from 1900-2130 (2100 on Sundays). Well-kept Ringwood ales and a regular guest beer are on handpumps. The bar is open from 1200-1430 and 1900-2300.

woodland to a further track where you bear left downhill with the yellow arrow. Where the track divides, keep right, following the grassy track ahead downhill between electric fences. The right-hand bank was ablaze with the mauve of thyme and mallow in early September.

Maintain your course into the dry valley, the track soon veering right passing an old brick and flint farm building and a slate-roofed barn, both to your left. A fingerpost then points your way across a stony farm track onto a grass centred track, which leads you uphill to the left of pasture. Beyond a small copse to your left, veer left to join an unsigned grassy route, which rises steeply through scrub into woodland. Arrows painted on trees make sure you do not wander off course, directing you out of the wood to a T-junction of tracks.

At this point you cross the stile in the hedgerow immediately in front of you, then bear half-left through a pasture, keeping left of the grassy mound in the centre to a stile situated in the corner of two wooden fences and beside a horse chestnut tree. Turn right along the lane that confronts you, following the brick and flint wall to Faccombe Manor to a road junction where you bear right. Those of you wishing to take refreshment in the Jack Russell pub, turn left at the clump of trees ahead, the pub lies just behind them.

Our main route remains on the lane, passing the gates to the Manor and onwards to the church of St Barnabas, which lies to your left. The tiny church enjoys a splendid rural spot, but was unfortunately locked when we tried the door and with no indication as to where one may obtain the key. The peaceful lane soon takes you through the cluster of houses that make up the estate village, passing the estate office that was once a chapel.

Shortly, bear right onto a waymarked track, keeping left at the sign stating 'Faccombe Estate Limited, Private Road', the metalled surface soon giving way to a wide stone and earth thoroughfare. Where this forks ahead, near a large manure heap, bear right, the track progressing downhill along the edge of a wood. The estate land is prime shooting country, the large number of pheasants roaming the tracks, fields and woods providing ample evidence of this country pursuit. It is sad to see that the majority of

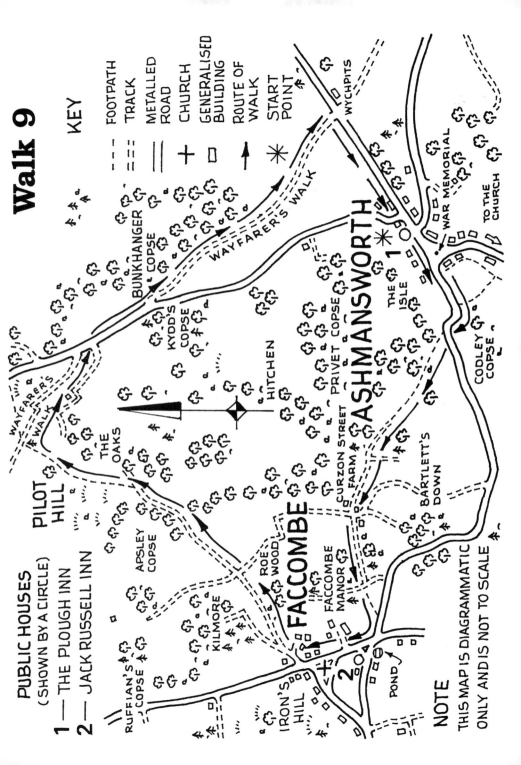

Walk 9

KEY

- – – – FOOTPATH
- = = = TRACK
- ‖ METALLED ROAD
- ✝ CHURCH
- ☐ GENERALISED BUILDING
- ↑ ROUTE OF WALK
- ✳ START POINT

PUBLIC HOUSES
(SHOWN BY A CIRCLE)

1 — THE PLOUGH INN
2 — JACK RUSSELL INN

PILOT HILL

WAYFARERS WALK

WAYFARER'S WALK

BUNKHANGER COPSE

KYDD'S COPSE

THE OAKS

APSLEY COPSE

HITCHEN

RUFFIAN'S COPSE

IRON'S HILL

KILMORE

ROE WOOD

FACCOMBE

FACCOMBE MANOR

POND

CURZON STREET FARM

PRIVET COPSE

ASHMANSWORTH

THE ISLE

BARTLETT'S DOWN

WAR MEMORIAL

TO THE CHURCH

CODLEY COPSE

WYCHPITS

NOTE
THIS MAP IS DIAGRAMMATIC ONLY AND IS NOT TO SCALE

Slightly tired footpath sign!

birds were without tails, obviously removed by the keepers to slow them down in flight and giving the shooting party a better chance of a hit.

Your route levels out at the base of the valley as you proceed ahead at a crossroads of tracks, to follow the edge of an arable field left-handed. Soon brace yourselves for a long steady climb up the valley side through woodland, before emerging out onto the open hillside. Persevere, for the rest at the fingerpost ahead allows time to savour the rewarding view into the combe and its folds of arable fields. Behind you, the scene opens out to encapsulate far-reaching views into mid-Hampshire. As you can see, the fingerpost points you uphill still, so there are better views to come. Your route heads across the hillside pasture between two clumps of trees to the stile on the horizon.

Climb the stile into the field beyond and peep behind you, for the full extent of your 'Hampshire' view. Proceed straight across the field on a barely visible path, keeping to the left of the copse in front of you to a log fence and fingerpost in the corner. A more defined path leads you through the next crop field. You are now on the highest point in Hampshire — Pilot Hill, 937ft — in the 'Hampshire Highlands'. A magnificent panorama slowly unfolds as you crest the top of the hill, across Newbury and Berkshire and beyond. A patchwork quilt of fields, hedges and forest confronts you as you drop onto a well-defined trackway — the Wayfarers Walk — which traverses the scarp slope.

From this stunning viewpoint follow the track right-handed along the ridge, eventually reaching a lane, where you turn right. To your left Highclere Castle can be seen looming above the trees at the base of the hill. When you reach a telegraph pole and a small oak wood on your left, turn left to the fingerpost and black arrow directing you along a muddy trackway, through the edge of woodland. The track soon becomes hedged, still with fine views, leading you to another lane. Here you turn right, following it the short distance back into Ashmansworth and your transport.

In and around the infant Test valley from Freefolk

WALK 10
Allow **3 hours**
5 miles
Walk begins page 61

Background to the walk

The crystal-clear waters of the River Test, one of the finest chalk streams in Europe, has long been known for its excellent trout fishing, however the iron-free water of the infant Test is also ideal for paper-making. Henri Portal, a Huguenot from France, established a paper-making mill on the river in 1712.

His first mill, the attractive weatherboarded Bere Mill still stands, and is located between Laverstoke and Whitchurch. Business flourished and Portal moved to a new mill in Laverstoke, where he started making a new watermarked banknote paper for the Bank of England in 1724. Portals had and still have a monopoly in this specialised type of paper; the original contract with the Bank of England survives to this day. The business remained in Laverstoke until 1950, when it moved to a mill in nearby Overton which Portals had opened in 1922. The present mill at Laverstoke dates from 1881.

The Portal family lived in Laverstoke House, built for the family in the 1790's. The ochre-coloured brick building is set in parkland and is visible from the B3400. Much of the housing in the estate village of Laverstoke and in nearby Freefolk has been built by Portals for its workers, none so unusual as the long row of half-thatched cottages, known as Manor Cottages. These were built by Lord Portal in 1939 in a vernacular Arts and Crafts style. Viewed from the front they are quaint and attractive looking and could be mis-

Maps
Landranger 1:50,000 Sheet 185. Pathfinder 1:25,000 Sheet SU 44/ 54. Map Reference of Start/Finish SU 483487.

How to get there
From Basingstoke head south on the M3 and take the A303 to Bullington Cross and then turn right onto A34. From Winchester follow B3420 north and join A34 for Newbury. Three miles beyond Bullington Cross leave A34 signed Whitchurch and go into the town centre. The Silk Mill has a large car park if you wish to start the walk here. For the Watership Down pub turn right at the roundabout onto the B3400 signed to Overton and Basingstoke. After two miles you will enter Freefolk, lookout for the pub signs directing you left. The pub lies a short way up the lane

on your left. Hampshire
Bus Service 30 (not
Sunday) between
Winchester and
Newbury via Andover
stops in The Square in
Whitchurch. You can
either start and finish
the walk here or catch
the Hampshire Bus
Service 76/76A (not
Sunday) between
Andover and
Basingstoke alighting
at Laverstoke Mill for
the short stroll to
Freefolk and the pub.

Pub facilities
The Watership Down
Built in 1840 as
Freefolk Arms —
nicknamed 'The Jerry'
as ale houses were at
the time — renamed
Watership Down in
1972 after Richard
Adams book. Walkers
well-catered for and
those wishing to visit
and park at the pub are
welcome. Bar open
1130-1500 and 1800-
2300. Four real ales —
the local King Alfred
brew being featured on
our visit. The changing
bar menu includes
filled jacket potatoes,
ploughmans, sand-
wiches, vegetarian
dishes, plus curry and
chilli. Food from 1200-
1400 and 1900-2100.
Splendid garden with
play equipment for
kids.

taken as being quite old, but the rear view of modern brick gives their true age away.

Set behind Manor Cottages on a hill is the Victorian church of St Mary built in 1896 and rich in decoration. Unfortunately, the tiny Victorian school set beside it has come on hard times for it was boarded up when we visited the church. In contrast, the tiny rustic church of St Nicholas hidden away down the lane opposite Manor Cottages may be redundant, but it is very much open for all to explore. It was built in the 15th century and well restored in 1703 as the roundel over the door indicates. Inside, classical reredos survive from the restoration and a 15th century wooden screen forms the front of a family pew.

The small town of Whitchurch, further down the river, developed after the establishment of a market and a borough back in the 13th century. It stands at what was once the junction of the Newbury to Southampton and Exeter to London routes and was an important crossing point on the River Test. During the coaching era the town was the first stop out of London and the White Hart, situated on the corner of these routes, was one of the major coaching inns. The author Charles Kingsley often stayed here when he came to fish the Test.

Whitchurch developed some industry, especially mills, utilising the river to provide them with power before electricity. Two flour mills existed, one of them being Town Mill, now a private residence which is passed on this walk. In Winchester Street the Silk Mill still survives, situated on Frog Island in the Test and is a splendid example of industrial architecture. It was built in about 1800 on the site of previous mills and was used for the hand-weaving of wool from 1816. Since 1830 the mill has been weaving silk and producing ceremonial dress and gowns for the legal profession and for academics.

Recently the Hampshire Buildings Preservation Trust has purchased the building, ensuring its future in years to come. The mill is open to the

The Red House
in Whitchurch dates
from the 16th century
as its flag-floored
public bar with large
inglenook indicates. A
lively pub offering
events, theme nights
and live music as well
as hearty food. Choose
from a value-for-money
bar menu or from the
restaurant menu and
blackboard specials,
served daily from
1200-1400 and Tues-
day to Saturday
evenings from 1900-
2130. Full Sunday
roasts are very popu-
lar. Excellent terraced
garden, ideal for
children — adventure
playground for over 5s,
toys for toddlers. Bar
opens 1100-1500 and
1730-2300 Monday to
Thursday, 1100-2300
on Fridays and Satur-
days, (usual Sunday
hours).

public all year from Tuesday to Saturday 1030-
1700. Visitors can see the historic looms working
and the restored waterwheel which was installed
in 1890. There are also some fine gardens to walk
around and a shop.

Walk 10.

Distance: *Allow up to 3 hours for this walk of five
miles, longer if you intend visiting Whitchurch Silk
Mill.*

Taking your leave of The Watership Down turn
right down the lane for a short distance to the
B3400 Whitchurch to Overton road, where you
turn left along the footway. At the end of the
cresent of half-thatched cottages — built by Portal
in 1939 for his mill workers — turn left if you wish
to visit the Victorian church of St Mary, visible on
the hill behind the cottages. Our route crosses the
road to join a tarmac drive waymarked to St
Nicholas Church. Cross the infant River Test and
follow the drive left to the charmingly rustic old
church. This partly-15th century, whitewashed
church, is now in the care of the Redundant
Churches Fund, but is well worth visiting for its
unusual fittings. You will find the key at Batt's
Cottage next door.

The White Hart is a
14th century coaching
inn with a bar offering
real ale from 1100-
2300, a spacious
dining area and 19
bedrooms. Good
snacks, salad bar
selection and restau-
rant dishes are avail-
able from 1200-1400
and 1900-2130 (2200
on Friday and Satur-
day).

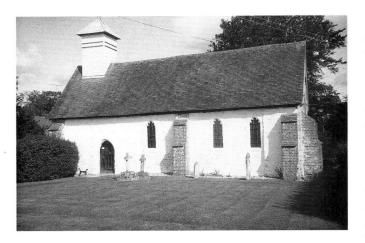

St Nicholas Church, now in the care of the Redundant Churches Fund, is worth visiting for its unusual fittings.

The driveway soon gives way to a pitted tarmac track beyond the entrance to Batt's Cottage, which you follow passing a brick and flint cottage to your right. Bear left onto a tree-lined, grass centred stony track, gradually making your way uphill out of the valley. Where the track bears left, veer right onto an arrowed path across a stile beside a field entrance. We could forego the stile as the entrance did not have the barbed wire, which is usually strung across its mouth. Beyond the stile disregard the muddy trackway to your left, instead, keep ahead along what was when we walked it a wide reinstated path through a field of crops. Maintain your course to the left of a solitary oak tree with a beautiful cameo view away to your right into the valley and the two churches, which seem to dominate the tiny village of Freefolk.

Your path soon bears right-handed gradually merging with the woodland to your left and a wide grassy track. In a little way bear off right to a wooden fence stile which you cross to enter a large pasture. Fine views into the Test valley can be enjoyed as you walk left-handed along the field's edge. To your right nestling in the valley beside the Test — which is not visible as yet — is Bere Mill, the picturesque weatherboarded mill in which Henri Portal first established his paper-making industry.

Shortly, where the hedged fence bears right, proceed downhill across the lush pasture to the base of the valley. Here you turn left to follow the hedged pasture to a stile in the right-hand corner. Climb the stile with verdant watermeadow to your right and walk along the base of the hill at the valley edge, with a line of trees on your right. The narrow, defined path leads you to a further stile and continues right-handed with an arable field to your left and lush tree-filled watermeadow on your right. If walking this path in high summer you will have to look hard through leafy vegetation to glimpse the crystal-clear waters of the Test. The river and its abundant wildlife is probably best viewed here on a winter's day ramble.

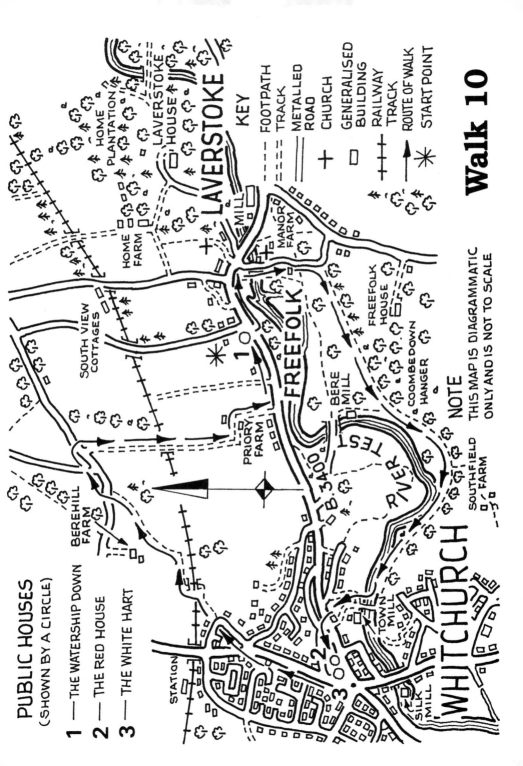

PUBLIC HOUSES
(SHOWN BY A CIRCLE)

1 — THE WATERSHIP DOWN
2 — THE RED HOUSE
3 — THE WHITE HART

KEY

— — — FOOTPATH
— · — TRACK
- - - METALLED ROAD
╋ CHURCH
▢ GENERALISED BUILDING
�꜔╋╋ RAILWAY TRACK
↞ ↟ ROUTE OF WALK
✳ START POINT

Walk 10

NOTE
THIS MAP IS DIAGRAMMATIC
ONLY AND IS NOT TO SCALE

LAVERSTOKE
HOME PLANTATION
LAVERSTOKE HOUSE
HOME FARM
MILL
MANOR FARM
SOUTH VIEW COTTAGES
FREEFOLK
FREEFOLK HOUSE
BERE MILL
COOMBE DOWN HANGER
PRIORY FARM
BEREHILL FARM
RIVER TEST
B.3400
SOUTHFIELD FARM
STATION
WHITCHURCH
TOWN MILL
SILK MILL

The trout for which the Test is duly famous for can be watched from the wooden footbridge in front of Town Mill, which you reach when you turn right where the path divides at the brick wall to the mill. Beyond the footbridge follow the gravel track to the right of Town Mill House, here it becomes metalled and runs parallel to a side stream of the Test. You shortly join the B3400, turning left along the footway into the centre of Whitchurch. The Red House pub and the fine old coaching inn — The White Hart — are situated on your right just before the roundabout.

If you wish to visit the Silk Mill, turn left at the roundabout and walk along Winchester Street following the road across the Test, the mill is on your right. Our main route turns right at the White Hart, following the footway uphill out of the village. You will have to cross and recross the road — which can be very busy with traffic — as the pavement ceases half-way up on the right-hand side. Turn right into Dances Lane, keeping left to pass the Police Station and Bere Hill Caravan Park situated on your right. Proceed ahead along a pitted lane which soon joins a metalled cul-de-sac and turning circle.

Your route cuts across the top of the circle to join a waymarked path to a stile flanking a metal gate. Climb the stile and keep to the right-hand edge of the pasture with open rural views towards Hannington Mast and north Hampshire ahead. If you have a dog with you, a few signs kindly ask you to keep it on a lead as you cross this pasture, which was grazed by a few sleepy cattle as we passed by. Three-quarters of the way down the hedge veer left across the field to a stile in the corner near the railway embankment.

Beyond the stile, climb another stile on your left beside a pair of metal gates and pass beneath the railway. At the end of the bridge, a further stile on your right leads you onto a path which runs parallel to the railway line, along the right-hand edge of a large arable field. Your path follows the field edge with Berehill Farm away to your left, eventually reaching a metal stile and a lane. Here you turn right, shortly passing a driveway on your left to Woodlings before proceeding uphill to a grass centred track which presents itself to your right. This old green lane affords good views south, as you make your way across the bridge over the Salisbury to Exeter railway line. The track becomes hedged as it descends towards Priory Farm, then in a little way where the hedge ceases, bear left and soon pass between a pair of brick and flint cottages and a large barn. Pass through a wooden gate and follow the metalled driveway downhill to the B3400. Cross over the road and turn left along the footway for a short distance before turning left onto the lane back to the Watership Down pub.

A chalk downland walk from Kingsclere

WALK 11
Allow **3 hours**
6 miles
Walk begins page 66

Background to the walk

The village of Kingsclere, once the largest parish in Hampshire is steeped in history. At the time of Domesday the village was simply called 'Clere', then from the 12th century it became an important royal estate, hence the addition of 'Kings' to its name. The area became a favourite hunting ground for various Kings of England until the 17th century, the lodge being located at Freemantle Park to the south of the village, where the television transmitter now stands. King John visited the lodge thirty-seven times, as is known by the inquisitions made on the village for the cartage of his wine!

Legend has it that King John on one of his hunting expeditions stayed a night in the village, possibly at The Crown or with some monks, and that he was impressed with the size and number of his 'bedfellows'. On leaving he promised the monks a weather vane for the church they were building. When it came it took the shape of a huge iron bed-bug, but it has also been likened to a winged dragon or a tortoise. It still adorns the tower of the restored Norman church of St Mary, a stone and flint building referred to as the Cathedral of the Downs.

The church has a memorial window depicting a racehorse, a tribute to John Porter an outstanding trainer in Victorian times at the famous Park House Stables. The stables produced seven Derby winners in the 19th century and two in the past sixty years.

Maps
Landranger 1:50,000 Sheet 174. Pathfinder 1:25,000 Sheet SU 45/55. Map Reference of Start/Finish SU535586.

How to get there
From Winchester head north via the B3420 to join the A34 for Newbury. Three miles beyond Bullington Cross you leave the A34 signed Whitchurch. In the village centre go straight on at the roundabout and head out of the village. Cross the railway, then shortly bear right for Kingsclere and follow this road for seven miles into Kingsclere. The free car park is signed to your right opposite the church. From Basingstoke follow the A339 Newbury road for approximately ten miles, before bearing left off the bypass into the village centre.

*Hampshire Bus service
302 between
Basingstoke and
Newbury stops in the
Square in Kingsclere
(not Sundays).*

Pub facilities
The Crown
*The pub is popular for
its bar food and in
particular for the choice
of two roasts available
on Sundays. Daily
specials such as liver
casserole and devilled
kidneys are extra to
the printed menu
which offers filled
potatoes, ploughmans,
sandwiches and
favourites like steak
and kidney pie. Food is
served from 1200-1415
and from 1900-2145.
The bar opens from
1100-1430 and 1800-
2300 and serves
Courage Best and
Wadworth 6X as well
as a guest ale. Groups
of walkers can be
catered for with prior
notice. The pub was
the scene of a particu-
larly violent incident in
1944 when the land-
lady of the pub was
caught in a fusillade of
rifle fire aimed at the
pub by at least ten US
servicemen from
positions outside the
front of the pub and in
the churchyard oppo-
site. Their intended
targets, two other US*

Kingsclere grew up at a meeting point of several important roads, and had fairs and markets in medieval times and a great diversity of employment in agriculture, brewing, ropemaking, tanning, milling and building. The stream that flows through the village once powered four mills, three of them still exist but are mills no longer. A brewery built in 1760 is now remembered only in the names of private houses — The Maltings, The Old Brewery House, Brewery Cottage and The Old Malthouse — but much of the ancient townscape remains — George Street has oak-timbered 16th century houses, Swan Street and North Street are lined with 18th and 19th century buildings.

Situated high up on the Downs is the attractive village of Hannington, part of which surrounds the village green which has a tiny spirelet covering a well. The green used to be two ponds, side by side and known in bygone days as 'Hannington Docks'. The church of All Saints is a mixture of styles. Two modern engraved windows are worth seeing, both designed and engraved by Laurence Whistler.

Part of our walk follows the northern section of the Wayfarer's Walk which traces the North Hampshire Ridgeway — a prehistoric track that exists between Basingstoke and the Vale of Pewsey in Wiltshire. On two occasions our route crosses the line of an old Roman Road — The Portway — which once linked Salisbury and Silchester and was used for military purposes.

Walk 11.

Distance: *allow three hours for a walk of six miles.*

Having parked your car in the free car park, which is signposted up Anchor Lane opposite St Mary's church, bear left uphill along the lane through a small housing estate. In a little way bear off left along a tarmac path, following the black arrow directing you to a walk-through 'stile' to a junction with a rough track. Here you turn left, shortly to enter the recreation ground. Bear half-right across the field, passing close to the swings, and head for the end of the chain link fence in front of you. Your route, now waymarked with the Wayfarer's Walk logo (WW) passes through another walk-through stile, to join a defined hedged path which affords views northwards across the village.

At the end of this path, bear right along an old stony hedged lane, where beyond a corrugated iron shed, you can enjoy uninterrupted views along the scarp face of the North Hampshire Downs, from Hannington Mast to White Hill and beyond to Watership Down. When we walked this way, the mature hedgerows were thick with spindleberries, holly, hazel, blackberries and old man's beard, and the grass-centred track was quite sticky with mud after the previous day's rain. Your track soon bears right downhill, the hedgerow making way for open farmland. Veer right off the track, the WW logo waymarking your route into the vast arable field. A well-worn grassy thoroughfare cuts its way across the field towards the base of the Downs, where at a pair of wooden gates it becomes an established fenced trackway, bearing diagonally left up the scarp slope of the Downs.

The gradient is not too taxing as the chalk and flint track gradually leads you between thick hedges and beyond to the crest of the slope. Pause a moment here and savour the panorama that greets you when you turn round and face north. On a clear day you can see miles, way into Berkshire and beyond. With rolling farmland in front of you, proceed along the track to where a blue arrow, painted on the supports of a water tank, points your way ahead along an established farm track, which follows the right-hand edge of a vast cereal field. For wildlife, this section proved fruitful. We observed four deer grazing in the centre of the field and a buzzard flew out of the trees and soared high above us for a while, in search of food. This track also affords views north-eastwards to Aldermaston, Reading and across to

servicemen, died instantly and sadly the landlady, Mrs Napper, died later in hospital.

The Swan
has a medieval hall and minstrels gallery, which form part of the lounge and bar. The inn was once an old posting house, supplying fresh horses for coaches and accommo-dation for travellers. It still offers rooms plus a variety of light snacks and restaurant fare. Food is served from 1230-1400 and 1930-2130 and includes a lunchtime sandwich menu plus ploughmans, homemade burgers, beef stroganoff, tortellini, soup and a range of five daily specials. On Sundays a roast is always available. Choose from treacle tart, bread and butter pudding or maybe summer pud-ding for dessert. Five real ales are served from 1100-1430 and from 1730-2300. Children are welcome in the bars as are dogs.

The Vine
at Hannington is situated high up on the Downs with views across the surrounding

countryside from its sheltered garden and attractive conservatory. Good food is a major attraction here; to accompany your ale try the burgers, ploughmans, chicken curry, aubergine and ricotta bake, salmon en croute, cashew nut and celery risotto, beef and mushroom pie or a choice of steaks. The menu is served daily from 1200-1400 and from 1830-2130, the restaurant is only open in the evenings. 22 draught beers are served, including at least 9 real ales of all strengths. The bar opens from 1200-1430 and from 1830-2300 with the usual Sunday hours. Children are only allowed in the conservatory area.

Hannington church.

the Chiltern Hills in the distance.

Your route passes to the left of a copse, bears left, then right round a crop field to pass beneath electricity wires before joining a narrow lane beyond some metal gates. Turn left along the lane into the village of Hannington. Follow the lane right-handed at the T-junction, passing the School House and a variety of other picturesque cottages — Abbotts Thatch, Old Post Cottage — to the village green. The Vine public house is further along the lane, beyond the green. Your route turns right along the edge of the green to All Saints church, which is well worth a few minutes exploration to view the Jacobean pulpit and the two windows by Whistler.

From the lych gate, bear left along the tree-lined gravel driveway to Manor Farm. Just before the gates to the farm your footpath is arrowed right along the wall, along a grassy path round a large black barn. Shortly, bear right between a hedge and wire fence to a small wooden gate, located beyond the modern barn to your right. A black arrow directs you left along the field edge, your grassy track soon becoming hedged on both sides. Maintain your course left-handed through the next field, to where your track passes through a hedgerow. Here, the vista south-westwards is magnificient, encapsulating the village of Overton, into the Test Valley, to Beacon Hill and to the rolling south Hampshire countryside.

Proceed a little further on this track, all the time looking out for a pathway to your right — through what was when we walked it a tract of long grass — which passes to the south of a scrub-lined old pit and head

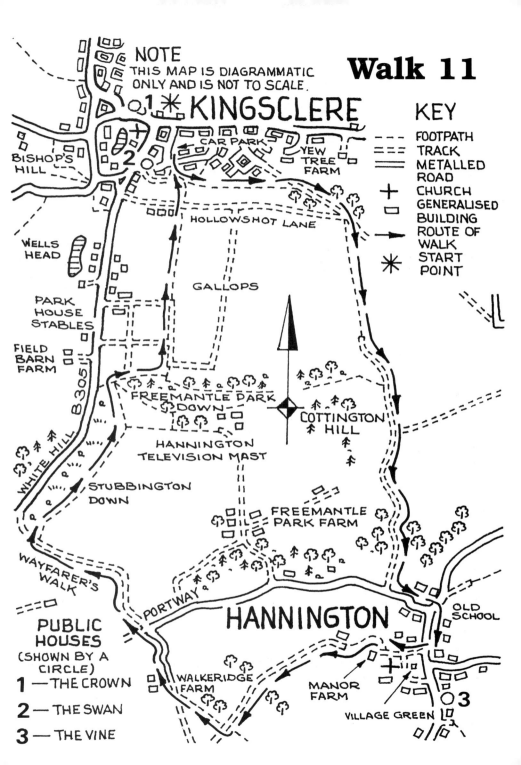

towards the building visible behind a line of fir trees. An old and very static tractor is parked where you join the metalled farm road, that precedes Walkeridge Farm. Turn right along this routeway — which happens to be part of the main Wayfarer's Walk that traverses Hampshire from north to south — and follow it to a narrow lane. This country thoroughfare follows the line of 'The Portway', an ancient Roman Road, which once linked Salisbury to the prosperous Roman town of Calleva near Silchester.

You now bear left along the lane, then at the fingerpost and WW logo, proceed right-handed along a grassy path between a mature hedge and a wire fence. Rolling farmland and open views can be enjoyed away to your left, as you make your way to a metal gate, beyond which you follow the defined track down the left-hand edge of a field, with Cannon Heath Down and Watership Down ahead of you. Pass through another metal gate and cross the stile immediately on your right into a crop field. Keep right-handed along the field edge, soon heading north-east towards Hannington Mast. When you reach the corner of the field, bear left, disregarding the stile on your right and proceed to the crest of the scarp slope and yet another set of stunning views northwards.

Cross the stile in front of you and begin the very steep descent down the scarp face, through scrub covered pasture. Beyond the stile in the fence at the base of the hill bear left, then shortly bear right with the black arrow to follow the established pathway along the bottom of Freemantle Park Down. Where the path veers left, maintain your course along the base of the wooded slope to where a narrow path passes through the woodland edge to your left, just beyond a large beech tree. Drop down onto a wide trackway and head north through 'The Gallops', an area of springy turf which is ideal for exercising the racehorses from the famous Park House Stables. Where the track bears left, keep ahead along a grassy track, fresh with the imprint of horses hooves, towards the houses at the base of the hill ahead.

On reaching the end of the long path through the Gallops, climb the stile situated next to a pair of metal gates, then cross the stony track beyond, to follow an arrowed pathway uphill between tall wire fences. This leads you up a series of concrete steps, to the left of a broken-stepped stile and back into the recreation ground in Kingsclere. This time you follow the left-hand edge of the field downhill to where you first entered the recreation area. Retrace your steps back to the free car park. For The Crown, pass through Anchor Yard to the Market Place, it lies across the road, opposite the church. For The Swan, follow Anchor Road to Swan Street and turn left, the inn is on the left-hand side of the road.

A stroll around Roman Calleva from Mortimer West End

Background to the walk

Mortimer West End lies at the northernmost point in Hampshire, exactly 51 miles from the most southerly point — Hurst Castle. It lies on an ancient droving route, which linked Wales to London. This straight thoroughfare running east-west through the parish is known as Welshman's Road, reminding us of the very long distances the Welsh drovers had to travel with their flocks.

A major part of our walk explores the Roman town of 'Calleva Atrebatum', which lies near Silchester and ranks highly among the noted places of Hampshire. Its earliest history tells of the arrival of a tribe of Gauls called the Attrebantes, who came here from Northern France. After the Roman invasion in 43 AD, Calleva grew into a prosperous town, its wealth generated through agriculture, and it soon reached the status of administrative capital. Many years after the main buildings had been erected, probably between 160-200 AD, the settlement was protected by the surviving earth ramparts. The facing walls which still exist today were added between 250-275 AD. No reason can be assigned for the abandonment of the town, which probably suffered a gradual process of decline around the 5th century AD.

The mile-and-a-half of walls that survive enclose the most complete plan of any provincial town in the Roman Empire, laid out in the rectangular grid pattern. The town was thoroughly excavated between 1890 and 1909, exposing the foundations of many buildings, defensive works,

Maps
Landranger 1:50,000 Sheet 175. Pathfinder 1:25,000 Sheet 66/77 Map Reference of Start/Finish SU633635.

How to get there
From Winchester follow M3 north towards Basingstoke, leaving at junction 6 signed A339 Newbury and Reading. Proceed straight across first roundabout for Reading, then at next roundabout take 2nd exit (Ring Road) towards Newbury and Aldermaston. When you reach the large roundabout ahead leave at the 4th exit, joining A340 Aldermaston road. Follow this for nearly 3 miles before turning right signed Little London. You soon bear left through Little London, remaining on the lane through Silchester, following signs for Mortimer West End.

Pub facilities
The Red Lion
(pictured right)
dates from 1575 as the
heavily beamed ceiling,
standing timbers,
wood-panelled walls
and two huge
inglenook fireplaces in
the one large bar
indicate. Cosy and
welcoming — espe-
cially in winter — the
pub offers a range of
real ales including
Gribble Ale and the
notorious Blackadder,
both brewed at a sister
pub in Sussex. You can
try these brews be-
tween 1100-2300 and
the usual hours on
Sundays. Food is
becoming increasingly
popular here; black-
board specials include
curries, pasta dishes,
hearty home-made
soups, ploughmans
and Red Lion speciality
pies — sweet and sour
beef, chicken and
mushroom or duck and
orange. The pudding
list may offer sherry
trifle or banoffi pie.
Appetites can be
satisfied between
1200-1400 and from
1830-2200. Children
welcome inside if they
are eating. Outside
seating in a sheltered
terrace to the front of
the pub. Walking
patrons may use the
car park.

a network of roads and what was probably the
earliest Christian church in Britain, before being
re-covered with earth. Calleva is unique compared
with other abandoned Roman towns, for it was
never built over again. Many of the treasures
unearthed during the excavation can be seen in
Reading Museum. A pictorial display of the history of the town at The Calleva Museum at
Silchester Common, is worth a visit. Our walk
conveniently passes the museum, prior to exploring the site.

Silchester's parish church of St Mary the Virgin, stands inside the old walls, near the east gate.
It was built about 1180-1200 and is largely
unrestored, with an unusual layout — a long
chancel and a short nave with aisles. Other significant features include 13th century paintings
and a fine old organ of about 1770.

Just outside the old walls, and an important
diversion from our main route is the Roman
amphitheatre, built in the 1st century AD. It has
been excavated and drained, so that its plan is
now very clear. The theatre could hold between
5,000 and 9,000 spectators on wooden seats
above the surrounding stone wall. They came to
watch sport, gladiatorial contests, wild beast shows
and public executions.

Walk 12.

Distance: *A good three hours should be allowed for this walk of four miles, as there is much to explore throughout the walk.*

From the Red Lion take care as you turn right to follow the often busy road north into the village of Mortimer West End. Pass the church of St Saviour on your right and proceed gradually uphill to a waymarked footpath, just beyond the 'Old School House' to your right. Climb the stile beside a wooden barrier fence, to join a bracken-edged path into a young predominantly larch plantation. The peaceful path leads you downhill, into what can be a waterlogged and muddy area, close to a stream. Negotiate the puddles, then bear left at a junction of paths to cross a railed wooden footbridge over the small stream.

The soft, pine needle covered path passes through scrub beneath some tall pines, which was alive with birdlife — nuthatches, finches, treecreepers and a green woodpecker — enjoying the warm autumn sunshine as we wandered by. Your route keeps just to the edge of the woodland — known as Benyon's Inclosure — with pasture visible beyond the fence to your left. A yellow arrow with footpath number '10', waymarks your path through the wood. Bear right with the '10' along a grass-centred track, then follow it left at a fork in the track, downhill on a stony track through undisturbed mixed woodland.

Your track soon bears left to cross a tree-lined causeway that divides a lake. Abundant with birds and other water-loving creatures, it is an ideal place to pause and observe the wildlife — especially if you have binoculars with you. Dragonflies were busy feeding, and taking advantage of the few remaining warm days were moorhens, coots, mallard and tufted duck. Our good deed for the day, was to help a magnificient freshwater crayfish across the causeway. It had been washed down a fast-flowing sluice into the lower lake and was desperately trying to return the way it had come, so we gave it a helping hand and plopped it into the quieter waters of the upper lake.

Leaving the water behind you, bear left where the track veers right and follow a track to a wooden barrier. Pass to its right, then at the end of a wooden fence to your left, beyond 'Little Heath', follow a path right-handed into woodland. Carefully wend your way through the trees and bracken, close to the woodland edge to a stile. Cross the stile into pasture and follow the right-hand edge, disregarding the two stiles in the fence as you make your way to a stile in the far hedge. Beyond the stile, turn right along a lane for a short distance, before turning left at the next junction for the Roman Museum. Keep left along Bramley Road, shortly turning left at a bridleway fingerpost onto a wide gravel trackway. The small green wooden building, housing the Calleva Museum lies to your left. Your route follows the pitted

Remains of the Roman town of Calleva.

track to a gate and stile beyond a row of cottages. Here you proceed ahead along a fenced muddy pathway, ignoring the stile and arrowed footpath on your left, to pass through a small wooden gate, which leads you onto the wall of the Roman town of Calleva. You now turn right through another small gate to follow a narrow path around the outside of the ancient bank and exposed wall. When you emerge from the tree-bordered path, remain on the grassy path between the flint-layered wall and a wire fence. It is possible to walk along the top of the bank, from which you have open views around the old town walls and of the spendidly located church of St Mary the Virgin, tucked just inside the wall. A path from the wall leads you into the churchyard, which is good place to pause and absorb the history that surrounds you.

On leaving the sanctuary of the church, follow the path back through the wall to the lane and turn left. To visit the Roman amphitheatre continue along the lane to where it bears sharp left at the post box. Pass through the wooden kissing gate ahead to view this well excavated and maintained theatre, which was built in the 1st century AD and used for sports. Return along the lane to a gravel track that precedes the driveway to the Old Manor House on your right. A fingerpost points your way to a pair of metal gates, with good views of the Old Manor and its fine small wooden barn set on

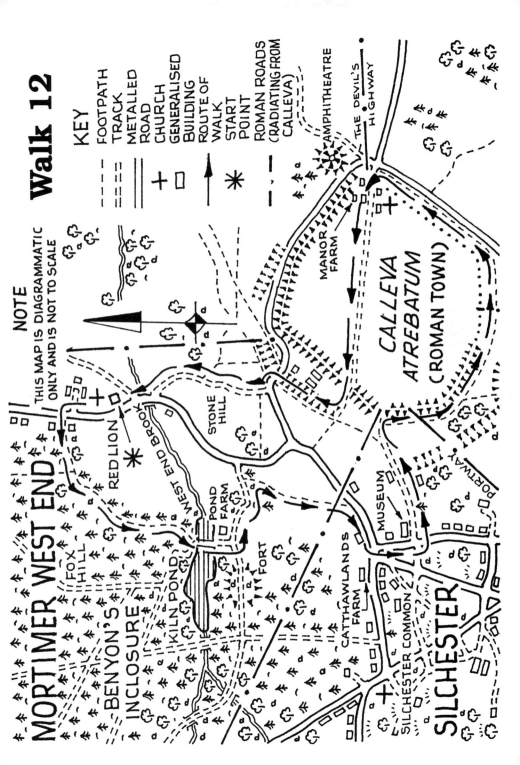

Church of St Mary the Virgin.

staddle stones. Pass through the wooden gate flanking the metal gates, then bear left along a wide fenced trackway, which cuts right across the centre of the Roman town. A splendid scene presents itself as you look across at the church; paddocks precede fine old barns that flank the attractive Manor and the ancient walls and embankments form the backdrop for the 12th century church.

The walls are visible all around you and when you reach the perimeter, keep ahead to the metal gates beyond it and enter a pasture. Your route crosses what can be quite waterlogged grazing land, to a wide gap in the hedgerow in front of you. Enter the next field and follow the mature tree-lined hedge right-handed to a stile and a lane. Here you turn left until a right-pointing 'byway' sign directs you along a muddy track through woodland. Remain on this — somewhat boggy when we walked it — thoroughfare, eventually reaching a road, where you bear right up the hill back to the Red Lion.

Exploring the Dever Valley from East Stratton

WALK 13

Allow **3 hours**

5 miles

Walk begins page 79

Background to the walk

The picturesque estate village of East Sratton is a true rural village, unspoilt by the passage of time. Both the park and village are of great architectural and historical interest and demonstrate the evolution of a village landscape which was directed by three eminent families — Wriothesley, Russell and Baring — during the 17th, 18th and 19th-centuries.

A manor has existed in East Stratton since about AD900, when it was owned by Hyde Abbey in Winchester. After the Dissolution of the Monasteries the estate was bought in 1546 by the Wriothesley family, who were responsible for first enclosing the park. In 1667 the manor became the property of the Russell family who set about landscaping the park with 'orchards, gardens and avenues, planted groves, wildernesses and other ornaments to adorn and accommodate this beautiful and pleasant scene'.

During the Russell's reign at the manor in the 18th century, the original heart of the village encroached very close to the parks boundary, towards the house. This village format soon changed when the Baring family acquired the estate in 1801. They twice extended the boundary of the park southwards, gradually erasing the northern half of the village. New uniform estate cottages, built of brick with attractive thatched roofs were constructed by Regency architect George Dance. Also built at this time was East Stratton Farm and The Plough Inn, as the village slowly

Maps
Landranger 1:50,000 Sheet 185. Pathfinder 1:25,000 Sheets SU 43/53 and SU 44/54. Map Reference of Start/Finish SU542399.

How to get there
From Winchester head northwards via A3090 to Kings Worthy where you join the A33 towards Basingstoke. After five miles turn right signed to East Sratton and cross over the M3. From Basingstoke take the A30 (or M3) and then take the A33 south to turn left over the M3. On entering the village follow the lane round a sharp right-hand bend, The Plough lies on your right a little further on, opposite the green. There is a car park behind the pub and space along the lane to the front. If parking is full it is possible to park at the green hall on your way back out

of the village near the church. Hampshire Bus Services 95 and 96 and County Bus Services 95A and 96A between Winchester and Micheldever or Basingstoke pass through East Stratton, except on Sundays.

Pub facilities
The Plough
is the epitomy of a true village pub, remarkably unchanged in the last fifty years. There is a warm welcome for all who enter its simple and unpretentious interior consisting of two small bars and a dining room. The food is all home-cooked and very much country fare, local game from the estate — such as pheasant, hare, partridge and venison — is often featured on the specials board. Other hearty dishes include vegetable soup, cottage pie, curry, rump steak, supreme of chicken and a variety of sandwiches and ploughmans. All the vegetables are grown in the pub garden. Sunday roasts are a very popular feature. Food is served from 1200-1400 and 1900-2215 except on Mondays. The bar is open from 1100-1430 and

developed southwards. Only the old school, built in 1846 and closed in the 1920's remains and a cross marks the spot of the original church, which was demolished when the new church of All Saints was built in 1890.

George Dance was also responsible for remodelling the manor in a classical style in 1803, the Baring's first improvement to the estate. John Baring had this destroyed in 1962 to make way for a 'modern' brick building, which looks bizarre hiding behind the mighty Tuscan portico which was kept at the front of the house. This architectural evolution of the village is traced towards the end of our walk.

The spelling of the names Micheldever has varied with the ages. In the 9th century it was 'Mycheldefer', in the 12th 'Micheldeura' and from the 13th to the 15th 'Mucheldever'. Up to seventy years ago it was written 'Mitcheldever'. It is thought to mean 'Much Water' but this is open to doubt. At present the only water is a small stream which eventually joins the Test, its true name is the 'North Brook, but is generally referred to as the 'Dever'. An indication that there must have been more water in the past is the existence of a mill — now a dwelling — at nearby Weston Colley, the river once driving the machinery.

The parish of Micheldever is believed to have been a royal estate in Saxon times and a manor is mentioned in the Domesday Book as having 83 hides (portions of land) and several Norman barons were sub-tenants. Since the Dissolution of the Monasteries the village has been linked with the manor at East Stratton, it being owned by the same three families. Sir Thomas Baring was created a baron in 1866 and chose the title Baron Northbrook from the name of a tithing in the parish. The majority of the village was sold off by the Barings in 1920.

Today the village is extremely picturesque, full of timber-framed cottages, many of them thatched. The church of St Mary is very unusual, in fact quite odd from the outside. The original early 16th

Bluebell Cottage, Micheldever

1800-2300 with the usual times on Sundays. An excellent range of ales from two Hampshire breweries were on offer when we visited, namely Gales Butser Bitter and HSB and Ringwood Forty-niner and their sweet and strong Old Thumper. Children are welcome in the pub, plus there is the green opposite for 'al fresco' eating and drinking, complete with tables and chairs and an old tractor, slide and swings for the children.

century tower adjoins a brick octagonal nave, designed in 1808 by the architect George Dance. Inside, the chancel has monuments to various members of the Baring family.

Walk 13.

Distance: *Allow up to three hours for this walk of approximately five miles.*

Having parked your car in the car park behind the skittle alley, follow the grass path in the right-hand corner to a narrow hedged path, which leads you to an earth and stone farm track, known as New Farm Road. Turn left here, the somewhat wet and muddy track — especially after prolonged rain — passing between hedges. It was here that we became aware of the incessant noise of the M3, beyond the hedge and field away to our right. The irritating roar of traffic was particularly bad due to the fact that we had begun the walk early evening on a weekday, at the height of the rush-hour.

After a short distance, at a crossroads of tracks, keep ahead with the yellow arrow on an old tree stump, directing you towards a wooden barn. The stony track bears right-handed around the farm buildings of New Farm, with the derelict remains of a brick house hidden among the undergrowth and trees to your right. Your route soon follows a grassy track beside a tall hawthorn hedge with pasture to your left. Climb the stile that flanks what is usually a barbed-wire fence across the field entrance, and turn right onto another established track — this is South Down Lane, bordered by an oak tree-lined hedgerow with open arable fields to your left.

Where a gap to your right presents itself as you enter another field, there is a neat rural cameo view with East Stratton church looming above the trees in the distance. It was at this point, being downwind, that we enjoyed watching three young deer frolicking around in the tall cereal crops, before they silently disappeared into one of the small copses that line the trackway.

Mind and soul numbed now — temporarily I am pleased to say — by the increasing decibels of the M3 roar, we quickened step to climb a stile beside a pair of metal gates. You now bear right onto a macadamised track to pass through the subway beneath the motorway. For much of its route in these parts, the M3 has been constructed through dense woodland or cut deep into the earth, thus reducing traffic noise and as in the case with our walk, not spoiling the rural splendour that prevails throughout our circuit.

Beyond the subway and a metal gate the track gives way to a stony, muddy track where water tends to linger beneath a dense tree canopy. As you dodge the puddles on your way to the A33 ahead, you will be accompanied by the barking of numerous dogs, caged thankfully, yet visible away to your right. Cross the A33 and follow the lane directing you to Micheldever, passing Highways Farm on your right. Shortly, you will be relieved of the hard tarmac with the appearance of wide grass verges on either side of the lane. The lane now looks like a private drive, straight, grass-verged, and with benches and lined with mature trees. During winter months it is not unusual to see 'Romany' travellers, with their colourful horse-drawn caravans camped on the grass verge, often advertising their services as knife-sharpeners.

Very soon you will enter the delightful, mainly thatched village of Micheldever. Look out for these characterful cottages — The Old Cottage, Perry's Acres, St Cross (dated 1540) and the chocolate box Bluebell Cottage which proudly displays a board stating that it was winner of the Best Thatched House award in 1980 and 1992. With the blacksmith's forge on your left, follow the lane right-handed passing the triangular area in the middle of the village known as 'The Crease', a name probably derived from the cross where four lanes met. At the churchyard, an old-style green fingerpost points your way up a few steps onto a path through the churchyard, shortly joining a tarmac path which leads you to the main door of what must be one of the oddest churches in Hampshire. St Mary's has a medieval tower and a modern nave added in 1808, yet the view from the main door is quite idyllic, looking out across arable fields into the gently rolling Dever valley.

When you leave the church, bear right through the churchyard and pass through a gap in the metal fence to follow a well-maintained grass path flanked by cereal crops and the large rear gardens to the village houses. Turn right when you reach the lane, cross the River Dever and enter the

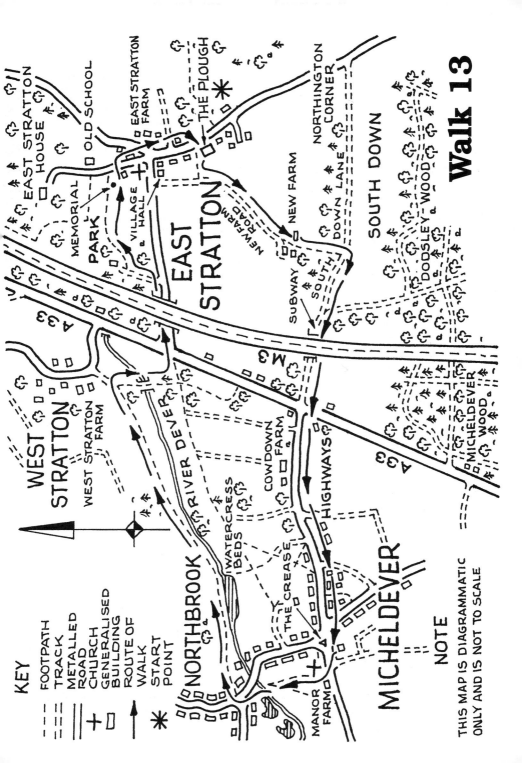

Walk 13

KEY

- - - FOOTPATH
=== TRACK
||| METALLED ROAD
✝ CHURCH
☐ GENERALISED BUILDING
↑ ROUTE OF WALK
✱ START POINT

WEST STRATTON

EAST STRATTON HOUSE

☐ OLD SCHOOL

EAST STRATTON FARM

THE PLOUGH

MEMORIAL

PARK

VILLAGE HALL

EAST STRATTON

NORTHINGTON CORNER

A33

WEST STRATTON FARM

NEW FARM

NEWFARM ROAD

SOUTH DOWN

DOWN LANE

SUBWAY

SOUTH

DODSLEY WOOD

RIVER DEVER

NORTHBROOK

WATERCRESS BEDS

COWDOWN FARM

M3

HIGHWAYS

MICHELDEVER WOOD

A33

THE CREASE

MANOR FARM

MICHELDEVER

NOTE

THIS MAP IS DIAGRAMMATIC ONLY AND IS NOT TO SCALE

hamlet of Northbrook. Your route now follows a waymarked bridleway on your right, opposite a lane signed to Weston Colley. The hedged path passes between cottages to a metal gate, beyond which you proceed straight across a large pasture, which was full of lively inquisitive cattle as we made our way to the stile in the wire fence ahead. With disused watercress beds on your right, follow the conifer tree windbreak heading for the solitary horse chestnut tree and a telegraph pole, along a visible narrow path through pastureland.

In the fading summer evening light we found this spot very peaceful; large numbers of rabbits emerged from the safe confines of the trees to feed and a Little Owl was out early, seeking prey as it flitted silently between fence posts. We stayed longer than we had intended, reluctant to venture back within earshot of the motorway. Time was against us so we pressed on following the grassy line and depression of the infant Dever, devoid of water as we passed by.

Beyond a metal gate, a well-defined track leads you through a scrub area before merging with a grass track with a copse to your left. The track soon follows the left-hand edge of an arable field to its corner, with a large house beyond the hedge away to your left. Keep right along the fields edge to a metal gate, beyond which at a T-junction of paths, you bear right through what can be a narrow nettle infested path through scrub, dotted with mature oak trees. Gradually rise up to another junction of paths, this time turning left along a well-defined path between lines of mature trees, eventually emerging out to the A33.

Cross the road and the motorway bridge beyond, turning left at the fingerpost directing you through a metal gate onto a stony track parallel to the motorway. Climb a stile just past the remains of a brick wall to a walled garden and follow the old iron fence on your left, trying to find the little used and overgrown pathway towards East Stratton park. A yellow arrow on a wooden fence post will soon restore confidence, confirming that you are on the right route. Soon bear right onto a track, then left to a stile and enter the Park. Proceed straight across the pasture ahead with the quite unusual modern 'manor' away to your left.

You shortly pass the memorial cross, indicating the site of the original village church, before reaching a stile. Turn right after climbing the stile, pass in front of the boarded old school and follow the metalled lane — once the main village street in the 18th century — and leave the park. The lane now passes some of the charming original 17th century thatched cottages — note the tiny post office, where transactions take place in the front room of the cottage — as you make your way up to the War Memorial. Keep straight on at the road junction, passing the telephone box back to The Plough and your transport.

Downland droving tracks and paths from Totford

WALK 14
Allow **3 hours**
6 miles
Walk begins page 85

Background to the walk

The group of dwellings known as Totford must be one of the smallest hamlets in the county, for it consists of the Woolpack, Totford Farm and a handful of houses, nestling in the picturesque Candover valley. Through the farm and across the valley to the pub runs the route of the Wayfarers Walk, a long distance path which traverses the heart of Hampshire, linking Inkpen Beacon in the north to Emsworth on the coast in the south.

Our circular walk incorporates the clearly marked 'WW' logo and black arrows of the Wayfarers Walk, following it south along old droving routes. Just beyond our starting point at the Woolpack, is an ancient cross-country route called 'The Lunway', which is known locally as the Ox Drove. The name Lunway can be found on charters dating back to Saxon times and can be translated to mean, a well-used track over the Downs (lun-common place, dun-down). A series of these tracks developed over time as long distance trade and droving routes for cattle and sheep, with The Lunway linking Old Sarum to Stockbridge, then progressing north of Winchester to join the Harrow Way, east of Basingstoke to Farnham. The importance of these old sheep droving routes is emphasized by the fact that Alresford market nearby, was one of the largest sheep fairs in the country, twenty-thousand sheep being sold there in 1885.

The highest point on our walk is Abbotstone Down, an area owned by Hampshire County

Maps
Landranger 1:50,000 Sheet 185. Pathfinder 1:25,000 SU 43/53. Map Reference of Start/Finish SU 571379.

How to get there
From Winchester head north via A3090 to Kings Worthy, turn left onto A33 towards Basingstoke. After two-and-a-half miles turn right at the Lunway Inn for the Candovers and follow a lane for three miles before descending into the Candover valley to the B3046 and The Woolpack which lies opposite the junction. From Basingstoke take M3 to exit 7 and the A33 and turn left under the M3 for Brown Candover and Totford. Or take the more scenic but slower route out from Cliddesden towards Alresford on the B3046.

Pub facilities
The Woolpack

once on old drovers inn where the sheep were penned in fields nearby while drovers 'rested' at the inn before continuing to Farnham market. It enjoys a peaceful location in the Candover valley, surrounded by open countryside. The part-flagstone open plan bar has a raised fire for cold winter days and comfortable seating around dark oak tables. People come from afar to sample the dishes from the regularly changing black-board menu that is served daily from 1200-1400 and Tuesday to Saturday from 1900-2200, on Sundays and Mondays from 1900-2030. Choose from cod chowder, moules or pâté and toast to start, followed by braised beef in ale, Woolpack sole, shepherds pie, chicken madras, steak and kidney pie or a range of steaks. For vegetarians, Mushroom strogonoff and harvester or vegetable pie may be on offer. Desserts include gooseberry crumble, crème caramel and spotted dick. A good

Council and used as a recreation area complete with picnic site and toilets. It was settled as long ago as the Iron Age, as the remnants of a hill fort known as Oliver's Battery indicates. The oval single-banked enclosure that exists today can be seen near the car parks. As with other earthworks in the county called Oliver's Battery, there is no evidence that it was used during the Civil War, but was probably named to commemorate the battles of 1664. Abbotstone Down is also an important area for downland flora and fauna, particularly for mosses and liverworts and the numerous deer which are often to be seen.

It is well worth lingering a while towards the end of the walk at the The Grange, an important house architecturally, being designed in 1804 by William Wilkins in the 'Greek Revivallist' style. The majestic porticoed building has a commanding position overlooking a lake and parkland and is owned by English Heritage, who restored the crumbling empty shell between 1970 and 1982. Good display boards explaining the history of the house, its links with the famous banking family — the Barings — and the long restoration work can be seen by the car park.

The estate village of Northington once belonged to the Grange and its church of St John the Evangelist — prominent throughout much of our

range of real ales usually includes the Hampshire brew, HSB from Gales.The bar is open from 1130-1500 and 1800-2300 and children are allowed in if they are eating. The inn has 10 ensuite bedrooms. Patron walkers are may use the car park.

walk — is worth the detour as you return to the Woolpack. Rebuilt by the Barings in the 1880's, it is very striking with a large tower and located in a beautiful spot, dominating the river valley scene. Inside are some fine chandeliers and candle holders and an interesting monument to the Baring family.

Walk 14.

Distance: *Allow at least three hours for this six mile walk, longer if intending to linger at The Grange.*

Your route commences on the Wayfarers Walk, which is arrowed left beside The Woolpack and is visible as you leave the homely confines of the pub. The metalled lane adjacent to the inn shortly gives way to a grass-centred stony track at a small white cottage on your left. Your track soon bears left-handed, passing farm buildings to become a delightful hedged green lane gradually rising out of the Candover valley. The occasional gate or thinning of hedge offers the chance to pause and enjoy the undulating rural scene away to your left. Behind you the prominent tower of Northington church dominates your vista.

The age of this fine old lane is indicated by the presence of many yew trees, planted for shade and shelter. This particular one is known as 'The Lunway', a name given to a series of tracks with Saxon and medieval origins, which developed as important long distance trade and animal droveways. Hazel, sloe and elderberry as well as yew line your route, and where the canopy is significantly dense, wet rutted muddy areas have developed, aided I'm sure by the passage of four-wheel drive vehicles. In recent years these old tracks around Hampshire have been opened up for all vehicles to use, including the ever-popular off-road jeeps.

Just as your imagination is conjuring up droving scenes of bygone days, you are brought suddenly back to the modern day as you emerge from the leafy old lane, to bear right-handed onto a concrete farm road. I hope the concrete flow is not allowed to progress down 'The Lunway' in time to come! On nearing some low farm sheds to your left, follow the 'WW' logo and arrow right-handed to join a wire-fenced metalled track (Spybush Lane), which leads you uphill towards a black barn and woodland. When you reach the barn linger a while, as we did, and look behind you — if you have not already done so — to savour the rural panorama that has unfolded quite unexpectedly. The gently rolling hills of the true heart of Hampshire lie before you, a mix of crops, pasture and copse from Beacon Hill in the north-west to Alton in the east.

Beyond the barn the macadamised lane gives way to a stony track, which shortly bears right-handed round the edge of a wood, then left-handed downhill with Swarraton Farm complex to your right. Where the track veers right towards the farm, proceed straight on, following a grass centred track which gradually bears left, uphill through a line of beech trees. When you reach the top of the rise pass through scrubland and newly planted beech trees, remaining on the track at a crossroads of routes before it gives way to a wide grassy path, which bears right-handed along the hedged fence of a crop field. To your left, open views across unspoilt Hampshire countryside can be enjoyed. On emerging from a mainly hazel copse, a blue arrow on a post directs you right through a grassy parking area, then across the B3046 into the main metalled car park of Abbotstone Down. The thirty-two acres of Abbotstone Down is owned by Hampshire County Council and used solely for recreational purposes, with many waymarked circular paths and a picnic area. Evidence of the Iron Age Hill Fort — Olivers Battery — can be seen as you pass through the car park.

Your route passes to the side of a padlocked wooden gate onto a stony track through the recreation area. When you reach the path to the toilets, bear left at the small post and black arrow, to join a grass path which passes between mixed woodland and lush grassland. The latter was abundant with wild flowers when we passed by. Pass to the left of a metal gate and join a narrow earth path through mixed woodland. As you emerge from the wood your path bears left-handed, affording open rural views westwards towards Abbotstone, once the site of a medieval village.

The well-established trackway follows a tree-lined hedgerow to a crossroads of routes, which precedes a farm building. A wooden fingerpost directs you right to 'Northington', the grass centred track climbing gradually uphill beside a mature mixed hedgerow, with peaceful arable scenes away to your right. Your views improve when you reach the end of the hedgerow, as you look westwards across the Itchen valley towards the downland around Winchester.

Shortly, enter scrubland where numerous 'Private' signs, nailed to isolated trees either side of you, make sure you keep to the well-defined thoroughfare. We walked this route on a balmy summer's evening and were privileged to observe several deer grazing peacefully in the neighbouring fields. The secluded tracts of woodland that are dotted around the large arable fields, coupled with the fact that few houses exist in the area, makes it a very popular haunt for deer.

A large hand-made footpath sign soon directs you through a mature beech wood to a stile at its far edge. Here a yellow arrow waymarks your route along a visible path through lush grassland, parallel to the woodland on your left. Climb the stile situated near the water trough, the arrows pointing you along the woodland edge to a further stile. Beyond this follow

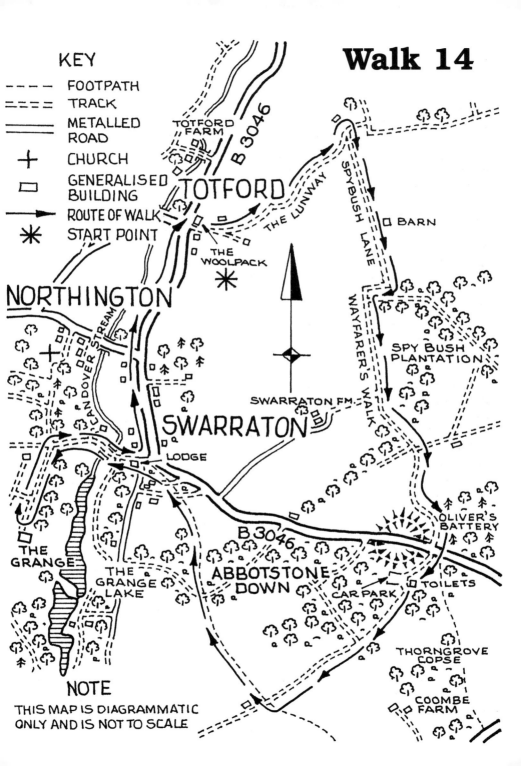

Walk 14

KEY

- - - - - FOOTPATH
= = = = TRACK
──────── METALLED ROAD
✝ CHURCH
▱ GENERALISED BUILDING
——▶ ROUTE OF WALK
✳ START POINT

TOTFORD FARM

B 3046

TOTFORD

THE LUNWAY

SPYBUSH LANE

BARN

THE WOOLPACK

NORTHINGTON

WAYFARER'S WALK

SPY BUSH PLANTATION

SWARRATON FM.

SWARRATON

LODGE

THE GRANGE

THE GRANGE LAKE

B 3046

ABBOTSTONE DOWN

OLIVER'S BATTERY

CAR PARK

TOILETS

THORNGROVE COPSE

COOMBE FARM

NOTE

THIS MAP IS DIAGRAMMATIC ONLY AND IS NOT TO SCALE

The Grange, an English Heritage property.

a gravel track right-handed, keeping right at the white sign onto a narrow woodland path, which leads you downhill to a driveway. A sign board leaning against the base of a tree to your left directs you across the tarmac drive and through the trees to a wire fence. Here you keep left, shortly to pass between two wire fences to a stile on your right.

Your route now takes you left a little way along a gravel driveway, then you bear right onto a narrow path into woodland. Climb an unusual wrought iron step ladder stile over fencing, the path eventually leading you to a stile beside a bus shelter on the B-road. Keep left beyond the shelter along a side lane off the main road, gradually rising uphill to a lodge on your right. Here you turn right entering the grounds of The Grange, an English Heritage-owned building, the exterior of which can be viewed between 0930-1830 in summer months and until 1600 in winter. A notice reminds you to keep dogs on a lead.

A pitted tarmac driveway — also a right of way — soon gives way to a stony track which crosses the Candover Stream — sadly quite dry when we passed over the bridge — and then again becomes metalled as it passes through fine parkland. The majestic Greek-looking facade of the Grange and its lake are soon visible to your left. When you reach a crossroads of tracks, turn left and follow the tree-lined driveway to the building. The house is empty, but its superb situation and tranquil atmosphere makes you want to linger for a while. The place to sit is on the steps beneath the porticoed front, for it overlooks a lake which is often teeming with ducks and geese, especially on frosty winter days.

Taking your leave from the Grange, retrace your steps back to the lodge and bear left down the lane past the post box to the B3046. Here you keep left to follow the road back through the adjoining villages of Swarraton and Northington — the church in the latter well worth the short detour — to Totford and The Woolpack. Care must be taken along this busy B-road.

Field paths and green lanes around Bentworth

WALK 15
Allow **3 $^1/_2$ hours**
6 $^1/_2$ miles
Walk begins page 90

Background to the walk

Bentworth lies hidden in the wooded, closely folded hills which form the south-eastern end of the Hampshire Downs. It is a sizeable village along one curving street with attractive large houses, thatched cottages and farms. It was once a royal manor in the 12th century owned by Henry I, King of England, Duke of Normandy and son of William the Conqueror. He gave the manor to his friend Geoffrey, Archbishop of Rouen and his successor Routrou, who financed the building of the large Norman church. In 1978 this French connection was celebrated when the 110th Bishop of Rouen visited the village.

The church of St Mary is interesting in that it is virtually all early-13th century. The pointed arches on the sturdy round Norman pillars in the church, are an expression of the Early English style which dominates the interior. There is a medieval font which has a charming pyramidal wooden cover dated 1605. In the churchyard there is a flourishing thorn, grafted from the Holy Thorn planted by Joseph of Arimathea at Glastonbury.

The oldest building, other than the church, is Hall Farm. It was built on or very near the site of a 13th century hall, and is a fine example of a medieval hall house. It dates from the 14th century, for it is known that after the owner William de Aule's death, his wife Matilda was granted the right to a private chapel, which still stands today at the south-west corner of the house.

The poet George Wither was born in the village

Maps
Landranger 1:50,000 Sheet 185. Pathfinder 1:25,000 Sheets SU 64/74 and SU 63/73. Map Reference of Start/Finish SU671402.

How to get there
From Winchester head west via B3404 towards Alresford, passing over M3 and shortly joining A31 following signs for Alresford and Alton. Remain on A31 which takes you through Ropley to Four Marks. Turn left for Medstead following the lane to a T-junction and turn left into the village. Turn right at the church towards Bentworth. The Star is in the village centre by the small roundabout. Bear right for The Sun which is situated down the next lane on your right. Parking is also available at the church, turn left at the roundabout.

Alder Valley bus services 214 and 215 between Winchester and Guildford and on Sundays Oakley Coach service 453 between Winchester and Aldershot both stop in Alton. Alight here to connect with Oakley Coach service 208 to Basingstoke which calls at Bentworth. From Basingstoke follow the A339 towards Alton, turning left for Bentworth beyond Herriard. For The Sun turn first left.

Pub facilities
The Sun
The building dates from 1635, at which time it was two cottages. Today, it is a classic unspoilt country pub complete with heavy beams, two inglenook fireplaces, brick and board floors and old benches and settles around rustic scrubbed tables. A free house serving four real ales — Wadworth 6X, Morland, Bass and Ruddles — from 1200-1500 and 1800-2300 and offering a range of home-cooked food including stews, pies, lasagne, chilli, vegetarian pasta, filled jacket potatoes, hearty ploughmans and french stick sand-

in 1588, and was well known for his satirical pieces about the government, which often got him imprisoned. His early work included pastoral poems such as 'Fair Virtue', which describes his time as a youth in Bentworth.

The parish of Wield probably derives its name from the German 'Wald', a wooded area. Others say it comes from 'Wold', or open upland or from 'Weald', it being at the western extremity of the Sussex Weald. Whatever its origin, the parish is divided up into two distinct settlements — Upper and Lower Wield.

Upper Wield consists of numerous thatched cottages, a large green and the tiny church of St James, which stands near a bridleway that was once part of the ancient thoroughfare from Winchester to Odiham. The church has existed here since the 13th century, although it was largely rebuilt in 1884. A Norman priest's door into the Chancel still exists and during restoration work in 1931 it was found to have its original oak bar still in position. The roof and west gallery are painted in effective fairground style.

Many deep wells were dug in medieval times, the only water available except for murky ponds. A treadwheel existed over the well by the entrance to Wield House Farm, while at the well now enclosed by the garden of the Manor, there was a donkey wheel. At King's Farm in Lower Wield there was a great hand wheel which lowered the bucket into the well; it is now in Alton Museum. Lower Wield has a collection of attractive thatched cottages and several farms.

Walk 15.

Distance: *Allow three-and-a-half hours for this walk of approximately six-and-a-half miles.*

From The Sun follow the lane right-handed towards the village centre, your route bearing round to a T-junction with the main village thoroughfare. Cross the road to where a fingerpost points your way along a macadamised path beside a flint wall. This grass edged path leads you to a small wooden gate, beyond which you enter St Mary's churchyard.

Leave the churchyard via the lych gate, passing the tiny village school on your right. Bear left when you reach the lane, following it round to the small green and The Star which lies opposite. Turn right across the green beside the solitary oak to a stile in the right-hand corner. At a footpath sign your route is arrowed half-left to a stile in the hedge ahead, beyond which you follow the well worn path through a crop field to a lane. A fingerpost directs you across the lane to follow the left-hand edge of an arable field northwards, towards Powells Farm. The pathway runs parallel to the hedgerow all the way to a paddock which precedes a modern building. Keep to the left of the paddock fence to a footpath sign waymarking you left, along a grassy thoroughfare between a hedgerow and a wire fence, with more paddocks beyond. When you reach the end of the fencing, turn northwards onto a muddy, grass-centred track, uphill towards a tree-lined hedge. A small white sign kindly asks you to keep to the path and to keep dogs on a lead.

As you pass through the wide hedgerow, look out for the hidden fingerpost on your left which directs you through a field entrance, then half-right along a visible 'dark streak' of a path across a large open field. The path leads you to the right of an isolated trough, towards a stile in the hedgerow in front of you.

Beyond the stile, you shortly bear right onto an established trackway, passing to the left of Rushmoor Pond. This tiny area of water lies at the convergence of four old droving tracks and would have served as an animal watering hole. Today it is quite overgrown, but still big enough for the family of Moorhens, who seemed quite content in this undisturbed spot. At this crossroads you turn left to follow an old hedged green lane, known as Rushmoor Lane. The heavy canopy of foilage

wiches. Food served from 1200-1400 (1430 on Saturdays) and 1900-2130. Dogs allowed in the pub, but children cannot be catered for as the pub is small with no separate area away from the bar. There are benches at the front of the pub. Walkers welcome to use car park if permission is asked first.

The Star

in the village centre by the green, is a village 'local' with an open plan layout — a public bar area with games and carpeted dining area. Bar opens from 1200-1400 (1500 at weekends and in summer) and 1900-2300, offering a choice of four real ales. Value-for-money pub snacks include toasted sandwiches, filled jacket potatoes, ploughmans, chilli and steak and kidney pie — available between 1200-1330 and 1900-2130. Sunday roasts popular in the winter months. If you are walking after parking, ask permission first. Walking groups catered for by prior arrangement.

allows water to linger in many places and the passage of farm vehicles churns up the mud, so we had to slowly wend our way along this sodden track.

Walking this on a wet winter's day, you will be relieved to find the stile in the left-hand hedgerow, located just beyond a wide gap in the hedge screen and escape from the quagmire. Your route now follows the hedge right-handed along the grassy edge of four fields, parallel to Rushmoor Lane. As the track veers right, bear left in front of a large shed and follow its concrete drive to a lane. A fingerpost — minus one finger when we passed — points your way across the lane onto a grassy path beside a hedge towards Lower Wield.

On reaching the corner of the field, climb the stile and drop down onto a lane opposite Sparrows Cottage, a splendid timbered thatched cottage. Follow the lane left-handed, passing Windmill Cottages. Disregard the waymarked paths on your left, as you round a sharp right-hand bend and continue to a stile in the tree-lined hedge on your left, just beyond a fine wooden barn and Kings Farm. A half-right pointing sign directs you along a defined path to a stile flanking a metal gate, which precedes a grassy track and a lane. Cross the lane, a footpath sign waymarks your route along a straight tree-lined track beside Drove Cottage. Emerging from the trees maintain your course ahead along the hedge left-handed to a stile, then proceed across the next field following the line of telegraph poles to another stile. Just before the stile veer left through a gap in the hedge, where a fingerpost points you half-left along a clearly visible path, towards the houses in Upper Wield. Your path bears right between the gardens of two dwellings to a lane.

You now follow the lane leftwards into the village centre, shortly passing Wield House Farm with its 300-foot well in the garden. This once had a treadwheel which took twenty minutes to raise the bucket. If you wish to visit the quaint little church of St James — a perfect example of a Norman Hampshire church — turn right on reaching the green.

Your main route follows the lane round the green, passing the old school which was closed in 1962 and is now used as a hall. Remain on this thoroughfare, passing the lanes waymarked to Alresford and Lower Wield, then on reaching a T-junction, you proceed across the lane to follow a signed bridleway that flanks a crop field. This grassy track affords peaceful rural views across fields and trees, prior to it being enclosed between tree-lined hedgerows. Here it has fallen victim to 4-wheel drive vehicles and deep water-filled ruts may have to be negotiated as you progress north-eastwards. Where a track converges with your route from the left, bear to the right to a T-junction of tracks and climb the stile in front of you.

A waymarked path leads you uphill, to the left of an old tree-surrounded pit through scrubland to the edge of an arable field. Bear half-left here to

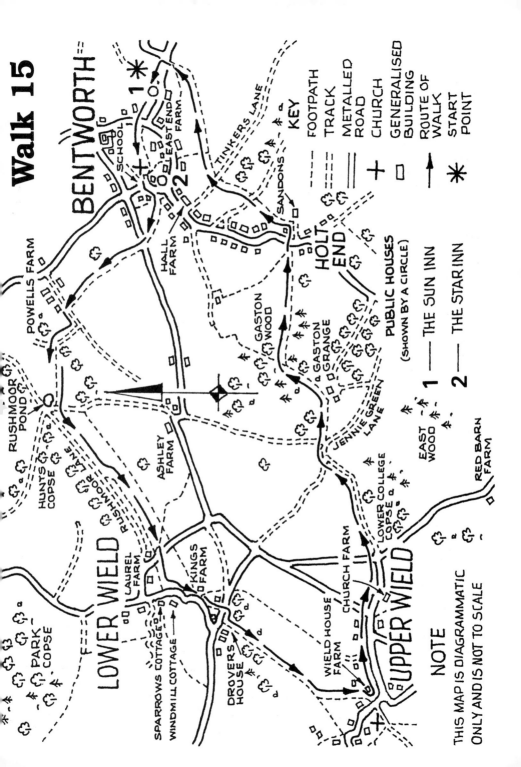

Upper Wield church.

a wooden gate hidden in the corner of the field, with Gaston Grange beyond the paddocks to your right. A yellow arrow directs you along the pad-dock fence to a stile that pre-cedes a pre-dominantly coniferous woodland. Your narrow pathway through the tranquil Gaston Wood soon merges with a wider track, here you proceed ahead to where an old stump, topped with yellow arrows, points you right along a muddy thoroughfare. Cross over the track leading to the pheasant enclosure on your left, onto a pathway which takes you to a small wooden gate on the woodland edge.

On entering a large pasture, a yellow arrow head waymarks your route half-left to a stile in the far corner. St Mary's church in Bentworth can be seen away to your left. Beyond the stile bear left, ignoring the stile immediately on your right and pass through scrub and thistles between wire fences to a field. This had been freshly ploughed when we walked this route, but a yellow arrow on top of the fence post angles you half-right towards houses and a metal gate. Climb the stile flanking the gate, bear right onto a lane, then left at the fingerpost along a stony driveway. Just as you enter 'Sandons' a slightly obscured yellow arrow points you left around the garden edge, through trees to a stile. Keep to the wooden fence on your left to a further stile, where you are waymarked ahead, following the right-hand edge of a pasture, downhill to the metalled driveway to Bentworth Hall.

Cross the drive via two stiles, maintaining your course north-eastwards along the left-hand edge of a field. Presently, reach a stile and cross a stony lane — Tinkers Lane, with Hall Farm to your left — and resume your route left-handed, through another field to a fingerpost and a stile. Disregard the path heading north, climb the stile in front of you and proceed ahead, this time following the hedge right-handed. Beyond two more stiles turn left onto a lane and follow this uphill back to The Sun.

Woodland tracks and hedged bridleways around Ellisfield

WALK 16
Up to 4 hours
6 ¹/₂ miles
Walk begins page 97

Background to the walk

Ellisfield is a small and scattered village, interspersed with woodland and copse, high up on downland in mid-Hampshire. The original village, now called Ellisfield Green, lies on one of the oldest routes in England leading from Dover to Stonehenge and on to Cornwall. It is now called the 'Harrow Way', its Saxon name being 'Hereweg' which means 'The Trade Route'. It was probably in use around 4,000 years ago and besides taking animals and nomadic tribes to food and water, such tracks were used to transport flints for making tools and salt for use as a preservative. In this area the Harrow Way is divided into a Winter or High Route and a Summer or Low Route. Ellisfield, in its elevated position and free from flooding is on the High Route, the Low Route passing close to Basingstoke at the base of Farleigh Hill nearby. It is thought that William the Conqueror would have followed the Harrow Way on his way to Winchester in 1066 after his victory at the Battle of Hastings.

Situated high on the hill behind The Fox is an ancient earthwork, known as 'The Camp'. Two stories are accepted about its possible origin. One tradition is that it was a north-western outpost of King Aella's domain, a Saxon who landed in Britain in 477 AD and became King of the South Saxons. Secondly, it is thought that the Camp may have originated in the Civil War, when nearby Basing House was beseiged by Cromwell, as was the city of Winchester. On a clear day the hills

Maps
Landranger 1:50,000 Sheet 185. Pathfinder 1:25,000 Sheet SU 64/74 Map Reference of Start/Finish SU632455.

How to get there
From Winchester head north via A3090 to King's Worthy where you join A33 towards Basingstoke. After 3 miles turn right for the Candovers beside The Lunway public house. At the T-junction in Totford turn left onto B3046 following it through Brown, Chilton and Preston Candover to Axford where you turn left signed Ellisfield. Turn left after a further one-and-a half miles into Ellisfield, The Fox lies on your left in one mile. From Basingstoke follow signs for Alresford, joining the B3046 through Cliddesden. Turn left at the pond for Ellisfield.

Pub facilities
The Fox

The original Fox Inn was located half-a-mile down the lane in Lower Common and moved to its present spot in about 1890. For many years the village post office was also on the premises, in what now is the kitchen. The inn enjoys a peaceful postion on a leafy green lane and a warm welcome is assured to all who enter its homely bars. Exposed brick walls, open fires, pine tables and chairs and comfortable wall bench seating charac- terise the relaxing lounge bar. The bar opens from 1130-1430 and from 1830-2300 for those seeking out the excellent range of seven real ales — Theakston Old Peculier, Gales HSB, Tanglefoot, Fullers London Pride, Wadworth 6X, Marstons Pedigree and the local King Alfred brew on our visit. To accompany your pint of good ale, The Fox offers honest home cooked food. Daily changing dishes may include venison in red wine, pork and apple in cider, carrot and stilton soup. Regular on the menu are steaks — 20oz T-bone! — salmon

around Winchester can be seen from the hill on which the Camp stands.

Domesday (1086 AD) mentions a church at Ellisfield, but the Church of St Martin was built during the second half of the 13th century. The earlier building was probably a chapel and stood in the grounds of the Old Rectory, now Brocas, on a site called Hallowed Litton. Litton is the Anglo-Saxon word for churchyard; so that a church stood in what was then Aelle's Field, named after King Aelle. When the Church of St Mary was built, there were two parishes in the scattered village; but the plague reduced the population to nine and it was decided to unite the two benefices. The church underwent extensive restoration in the late 19th century and the Gothic Revival tower was built during that time, replacing a wooden structure that existed over the nave in which five bells were hung. The avenue of pleached limes which forms an arcade between the lychgate and the church door was planted in 1897.

An unusual feature of the church is the strange shape of its weathervane. It is in the form of a louse and has inspired several legends to explain how it came into being. One is that a curate found his lodging so louse-ridden that he presented the church with the weathervane to commemorate his discomfort.

Returning through Ellisfield at the end of our walk we cross College Lane, which has a large farm situated further down the lane, known as College Farm. Much of this land was once the property of Winchester College and it is thought that at one time the farm was used as an isolation retreat for college boys to escape plague and typhoid when there were outbreaks in Winchester.

Walk 16.

Distance: *Allow up to four hours for this six-and-a-half mile walk.*

and trout, plus hearty snacks such as granary sandwiches, ploughmans, filled pittas and potatoes. Appetites can be satisfied daily between 1200-1400 and Tuesday to Sunday evenings from 1900-2130. Children under 14 are not allowed inside. There is a pleasant garden for al fresco eating and drinking.

From The Fox follow the lane north to where Green Lane bears right uphill. Here you cross the stile to your left, located beside a field entrance strung with barbed wire into a pasture. A fingerpost points you half-right, uphill towards woodland. The earthwork marking the area known as The Camp lies away to your left. Although Winchester is not visible, the open views south towards Winchester can be appreciated from this vantage point. Climb the stile which precedes the wood and join a wide grass path which leads you through Bedlam Plantation, passing some disued pits to your left. Shortly, the bramble and bracken edged path brings you to a stile at the woodland edge, from which there are views down the dry combe called Bedlam Bottom.

Your route now follows the pasture right-handed downhill to the isolated and thatched Keepers Cottage in the base of the combe. When you reach a grass-centred stony track follow it south away from the cottage, along the valley bottom to a metal gate. If closed, climb the stile in the fence and maintain your course through this tranquil, unspoilt combe. Walking through this sheltered wooded scene, it is hard to believe that you are in Hampshire, it looks and feels like a steep-sided and forested Welsh valley. As we sauntered this way pheasants were in abundance, running in all directions. Keep right when you arrive at a fork in the track, a sign notifies you that the left-hand track is not a pulic right of way.

The wooded valley sides soon narrow down and your track becomes tree-lined as you begin to emerge from the combe. Beyond an old shed your route becomes fenced with an arable field to your right. The track here is liable to be wet and muddy in places after rain, as it collects in the ruts created by the passage of farm vehicles. Eventually bear right by a low thatched house onto a narrow lane, then turn left in a little way onto a waymarked bridleway. At the time we walked this path (September) the early stages were well-defined, as the narrow hedge-bordered route gently climbed uphill. Gradually it deteriorated, becoming thick with vicious tall nettles, due to lack of use and general upkeep. Armed as we were with a stick, we managed to keep most of the nettles at bay, away from our bare legs. Persevere up to a small wooden gate and enter a pasture, with Moundsmere Farm to your left. Follow the wire fence right-handed to another wooden gate, beyond which you bear left along the concrete drive towards the cream-painted farmhouse. Pass through the farmyard, keeping to the left of the Estate Office. Beyond the farm you will be able to glimpse Moundsmere Manor to your right. You now follow the tree-lined macadamised drive away from the manor to a lane.

Cross straight over the lane to where a bridleway fingerpost directs you into thick woodland — Preston Oak Hills — via what was a very sodden and muddy track. Little sunlight seems to penetrate deep into the wood, to dry out this peaceful thoroughfare. The regular passage of horses from the Manor's stables and vehicle wheels maintain the uneven and often rutted surface. Walkers, however have managed to weave narrow paths around the worst of the muddy tracts. The damp woodland air within this fine mixed forest of mature oaks, birch, beech and horse chestnut, aids the growth of lush grass along the track and much of the floor is bracken-covered. Birdlife abounds, we saw a variety of songbirds plus goldcrest, long-tailed tits and a nuthatch.

As you near the far end of the wood, where an arable field presents itself to your left, turn left to follow a visible path through the trees, along the woodland edge. At the bottom of the hill turn left along Axford Road — an underground stream follows the line of the road and for many years houses had to pump the water from this source — then turn almost immediately right onto a hedged track that rises gently uphill. Where the track bears right, keep ahead, the old grass centred lane passing between a line of trees. Keep your eyes peeled as you make your way northwards, for you stand a good chance of seeing deer, as they make their way between the many copses that exist around Ellisfield.

Maintain your course north, across two crossroads of tracks, to where the tree-lined, mud and stone track passes between two houses to a lane. Follow Bell Lane left-handed past Kit Lane House to a T-junction with College Lane with the driveway to Ellisfield Grange directly in front of you. To your left, a fingerpost beside the post box points you across the lane into a crop field. Here you follow the edge of the field right-handed beside woodland. Where the woodland edge angles sharp right, look out for the worn path that bears half-left across the field, towards some buildings and a stile in the corner of the field. Climb the stile — broken stepped when we encountered it — and drop down to the junction of Furzen Lane and Church Lane. Follow the sign waymarking your route to the church,

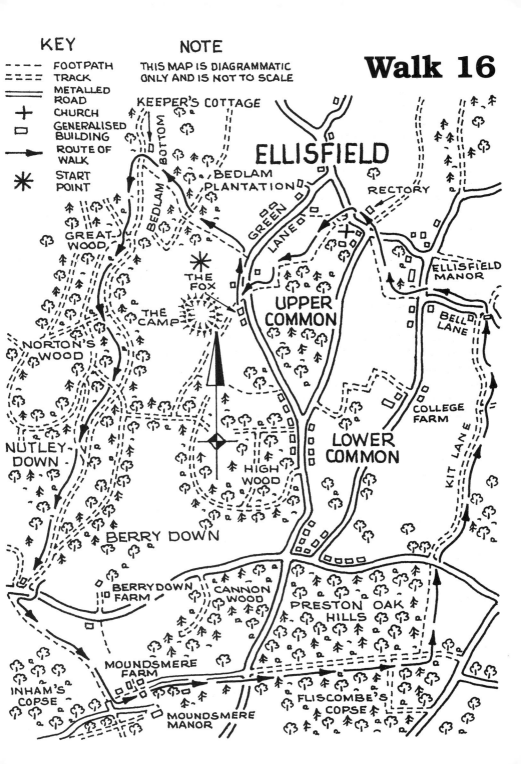

Walk 16

KEY

- - - - FOOTPATH
- = = = TRACK
- ———— METALLED ROAD
- + CHURCH
- ▭ GENERALISED BUILDING
- ——▶ ROUTE OF WALK
- ✳ START POINT

NOTE

THIS MAP IS DIAGRAMMATIC ONLY AND IS NOT TO SCALE

KEEPER'S COTTAGE

BEDLAM BOTTOM

ELLISFIELD

BEDLAM PLANTATION

RECTORY

GREEN LANE

GREAT WOOD

THE FOX

THE CAMP

ELLISFIELD MANOR

UPPER COMMON

BELL LANE

NORTON'S WOOD

COLLEGE FARM

NUTLEY DOWN

HIGH WOOD

LOWER COMMON

KIT LANE

BERRY DOWN

BERRYDOWN FARM

CANNON WOOD

PRESTON OAK HILLS

MOUNDSMERE FARM

INHAM'S COPSE

MOUNDSMERE MANOR

FLISCOMBE'S COPSE

Ellisfield church

passing the village hall on your way to the church of St Martin.

The church enjoys a charming position in front of the Old Manor, its neat churchyard enclosed by a wooden fence of hew beams. This fence is a modern provision reviving an old custom: each family in the parish is asked to supply a section of the fence and the incumbent supplies the gate. Church Registers have post and rail donor lists as far back as 1589. On leaving the church and lych gate via the fine avenue of limes, bear left round the churchyard wall, to follow the waymarked path along a hedged green lane. Your route skirts the churchyard to a stile, with the manor and church to your left. Climb the stile and the one beyond into a pasture. You now bear half-right across the field to a stile that flanks the woodland edge ahead. Beyond this, your path follows the line of the wood, crossing a further two stiles. At the end of the wood, cross the stile on your left and angle right, downhill across pasture following the line of telegraph poles. Soon the pub sign of The Fox becomes visible above the hedge prior to you crossing a stile beside a metal gate onto the lane opposite the pub.

Canal, river and downland paths from Upton Grey

WALK 17

Allow **4 $^1/_2$ hours**

7 miles

Walk begins page 103

Background to the walk

In Saxon times Upton Grey was known as Aoltone, then later as Upetone and Upetona. The second part of its name comes from the De Grey family who owned the manor from the 13th to the 15th century. It is a most attractive village with a pond — complete with ducks — by the crossroads, surrounded by old brick and timber framed cottages.

At the end of the last century this farming village had three shops, two shoemakers, two blacksmiths, a baker, a wheelwright, a tailor, a maltster and a publican and was a thriving community. Today, buildings such as The Old Post Office, The Old School House and The Forge provide evidence of busier times, yet the village still retains its true village spirit despite many of the villagers commuting out of the village for work.

At the top of the delightful main street is St Mary's church, which dates back to Norman times and is quite unusual in its arrangement. The wide brick north aisle was added in 1715 and is out of proportion to the small nave and the even smaller 12th century chancel. The result is that anyone sitting in the north aisle would not be able to see the altar, which is round the corner.

At two points on this walk you will cross the Basingstoke Canal, which was originally conceived as a major commercial route between London and North Hampshire. It was completed in 1794 and climbed 37 miles through Surrey to Hampshire with the aid of 29 locks and a 1,230 yard tunnel.

Maps
Landranger 1:50,000 Sheet 186. Pathfinder 1:25,000 Sheets SU 64/74 and SU 65/75 Map Reference of Start/Finish SU700482.

How to get there
From Winchester head north along M3 towards Basingstoke. Leave the motorway at Junction 6 to A339 then at the first roundabout, you take the third exit, the A30 for Hook. In a short distance you turn right for Tunworth and cross the motorway. At a T-junction turn left, following the lane through Tunworth to Upton Grey. Go down the main village street to the pond, then bear left for the Hoddington Arms.

Pub facilities
Hoddington Arms
Ever-popular and busy most lunchtimes with business clientele from

Basingstoke, the draw being the excellent value home-cooked food that is available from 1200-1400 and in the evenings from 1930-2130 (2100 on Sundays). The daily changing blackboard menu ranges from Goan style pork curry, jugged beef steak, canelloni, steak and kidney pie to a choice of 6 ploughmans and sandwiches. Sticky toffee pudding or treacle sponge are on the sweet list. Well-kept Morland ales and a guest beer can be sampled between 1100 and 1430 and from 1800-2300 (1130-1430 and 1900-2300 on Saturdays), usual times on Sundays. Family room for rainy days and large garden for children the on sunny days. Walkers welcome to use the car park if permission is asked first.

Fox and Goose

Situated a stone's throw from the Basingstoke Canal in Greywell is this welcoming ale house serving Ushers and good bar snacks. Curries, pies, grills, steaks as well as sandwiches and toasties can be ordered

The Hoddington Arms

Barges transported timber, coal and grain as towns grew up alongside it, but the coming of the railways heralded the gradual decline of the canal as a commercial routeway. In its heyday it transported materials for the construction of the London to Southampton railway, opened to Basingstoke in 1839, carried bricks and timber to build the military camp at Aldershot in 1854 and served the brickworks at Up Nately in 1896. During the First World War it was used to shift munitions, then after the collapse of Greywell Tunnel in 1934 the western end of the canal began to deteriorate and silt up.

Greywell Tunnel, built in 1792, became the longest tunnel in the south of England, being nearly a mile long. Like many others it had no towpath, so barges had to be 'legged' through by bargees lying on their backs and pushing with their feet against the tunnel roof, while the horses went overland.

The Surrey and Hampshire Canal Society was formed in 1966 to stop the decay. Restoration work was completed and the canal reopened in 1991. The 32 miles from the River Wey navigation junction to the Greywell Tunnel is now in use again but as a leisure amenity.

Since the collapse of the tunnel roof it has become one of the most important bat roosts in Britain; it has been estimated that there are about

2,000 bats of five different species living in the tunnel, including Natterer's bats and Daubenton's or water bats. It is quite an experience at dusk each evening, to watch the bats leave the tunnel for a night's feeding. You can reach the entrance by taking a waymarked path off our main route in the village centre.

The village of Greywell is attractively located beside the River Whitewater with many 17th century brick and timber cottages. The medieval St Mary's church stands in a delightful spot within a few yards of the river. Of particular note is the 16th century wooden rood screen and the circular stair-turret that gave access to the rood.

between 1200-1400 and from 1900-2200, except on a Sunday and Monday evening. The bar is open from 1100-1430 and from 1730-2300, with normal Sunday hours. Well-behaved children welcome in the bar and the garden has a climbing frame and swings. Ask the landlord if you plan to park and walk from the pub.

Walk 17.

Distance: *Allow four hours for this seven mile walk.*

Leaving The Hoddington Arms car park turn left along the lane towards the village centre. At the picturesque scene of pond, ducks and old cottages, turn right to follow the main village street, uphill towards the church, passing the Post Office, village hall and well-stocked store. Look out for the Norwich Union fire mark on 'Spinners' to your right. Before the fire brigades we know today, insurance companies had their own private fire brigades to protect clients' properties. If a fire occured the clearly visible fire mark identified which insurance fire brigade should be called out. Our stroll through this attractive cameo of village life culminates at the church of St Mary.

When you leave the churchyard, retrace a few steps to the waymarked footpath on your left, arrowed between two dwellings. The narrow path leads you to the rear of Manor Farm and its fine garden, bearing round to an arable field with the farm building to your left. Keep ahead between a line of trees and a wire fence, shortly to bear right onto a track, which takes you away from the farm, along the field edge to a lane. Cross the lane and stile in front of you, then bear half-right across a paddock to another stile in the fence, beyond which you maintain direction passing to the right of a bungalow. Climb the stile — broken stepped when we negotiated it — that flanks a metal gate and walk along a grassy track to a metalled lane.

Here you turn left briefly, keeping straight on where the lane veers sharp left, to join a stony farm track which leads you out into open countryside. Your views are only interrupted by the tall Basingstoke office buildings that loom above the trees to your left. When you reach a T-junction of tracks, turn right to follow an mature tree-lined green lane to a crossroads of tracks known as 'Five Lanes End'. Lined with beech trees and high up on downland, this junction is where five old droving routes once converged. Your route follows the second track on your left, round the main beech tree with its exposed roots. Where this bears left, look out for the fingerpost pointing you right into crop fields. Keep to the left of the hedge in front of you, following the field edge to a stile in the hedge.

Beyond the stile, proceed ahead along the left-hand edge of two pastures to a gate and macadamised lane. It was at this point that a sparrowhawk swooped out of the sky to catch some prey in the field opposite and to our surprise, remained in the open field feeding, allowing us a superb view through the binoculars. Climb the stile across the lane and keep ahead through the pasture, to a further stile that precedes some trees. Your narrow path now passes between a mature hedge and a wire fence, towards Up Nately church which soon comes into view. At a T-junction of paths beyond a stile, turn right to a metal gate, where a fingerpost directs you left-handed along the field edge to another stile, located in the hedge close to the churchyard. After crossing the stile a narrow path leads you around the perimeter of the churchyard to a road. Rest a few minutes at the tiny Norman church of St Stephen — rebuilt in 1844 — but still retaining a Norman door, chancel arch and 15th century timber roof.

Your route crosses the road to follow the waymarked path along Heather Lane, where you soon pass over the overgrown most westerly surviving part of the Basingstoke Canal. The stony lane curves right with large properties lining both its sides, until it bears left into the driveway of Woodlands. Here you keep ahead to join a narrow path through woodland, shortly turning right along a pathway — parallel to a deeply rutted and muddy trackway — downhill to a bridge over the canal. Beyond the canal a stony track takes you to a metalled lane, with Eastrop Farmhouse to your right. Follow the lane gently uphill, bearing sharp left, then where the lane turns right proceed straight on at the bridleway fingerpost, along a hedged path. A notice soon informs you that the woodland area to your left is a conservation area and that dogs must be kept on a lead. Greywell Tunnel — all 1,230 yards of it — lies beneath this tract of woodland.

Your path leads you along the edge of this peaceful mixed woodland, which was rich in wildlife, especially with numerous species of songbirds. When you reach a crossroads of tracks, proceed ahead, the path gradually rising uphill to a wooden gate. Beyond this, bear half-right emerging out into pasture and keep left along a line of oak trees to a fingerpost, situated in front of a large tree. Disregard the route right, downhill to a small metal gate, instead bear half-right across the field with the grand Greywell Hill House behind you, to a stile in the corner. Climb the stile, bear right, the hedged path gradually taking you downhill to a gate and a lane, where you

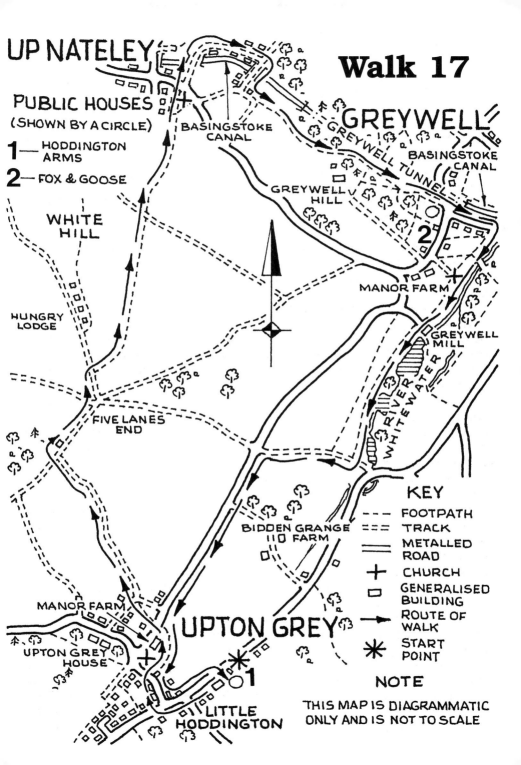

UP NATELEY

PUBLIC HOUSES
(SHOWN BY A CIRCLE)

1 — HODDINGTON
ARMS

2 — FOX & GOOSE

WHITE
HILL

HUNGRY
LODGE

BASINGSTOKE
CANAL

Walk 17

GREYWELL

GREYWELL TUNNEL

BASINGSTOKE
CANAL

GREYWELL
HILL

2

MANOR FARM

GREYWELL
MILL

RIVER WHITEWATER

FIVE LANES
END

KEY

- - - FOOTPATH

= = = TRACK

——— METALLED
ROAD

+ CHURCH

▢ GENERALISED
BUILDING

→ ROUTE OF
WALK

✳ START
POINT

BIDDEN GRANGE
FARM

MANOR FARM

UPTON GREY
HOUSE

UPTON GREY

1

LITTLE
HODDINGTON

NOTE

THIS MAP IS DIAGRAMMATIC
ONLY AND IS NOT TO SCALE

Upton Grey church

bear right into the village of Greywell.

The Fox and Goose lies a short way along the lane on your right, your main route bearing left towards Odiham. If you wish to view the fully restored Basingstoke Canal and the entrance to Greywell Tunnel, cross the stile on your left, waymarked to the Canal. Return to the lane and bear left through the village. Beyond 'The Old Chapel' and just before a house called 'The Ford' take the arrowed path on your right, between wooden garden fences to a stile. Cross the stile into meadowland beside the River Whitewater, your route running parallel with the river on a defined path to Greywell church ahead. Pass through a swing gate into the churchyard, the idyllic meadow setting of St Mary's and its unusual internal features make it an ideal spot to rest and linger awhile.

Refreshed, follow the path to the right of the church, leaving the churchyard via a stile, with watermeadow and reeds to your left. Beyond a further stile, your path passes through scrub before duckboards lead you to the edge of the River Whitewater. Again, this is a most tranquil scene in which to pause and savour this serene river and its wildlife. Sitting on one of the small benches on the grassy bank we observed dragonflies skimming the water, tiny wrens flitted through the willows along the water's edge and odd noises and rustlings could be heard among the reeds, probably made by small creatures and birds. Shortly, your path bears right and Greywell Mill comes into view, complete with waterwheel.

When you reach the trackway in front of the mill, turn right for a little way before bearing left at the fingerpost, beyond wooden fencing, up a few steps and over a stile into pasture. Here you follow the left-hand edge of the field, with willow and reed beyond the fence, signifying the course of the river. Maintain this route across two stiles and as many fields to a stile flanking a metal gate. Turn right to follow a hedge bordered, grass centred track gently climbing uphill to a narrow lane, where you turn left, remaining on this relatively traffic-free lane back towards Upton Grey. Shortly after passing some houses to your right, a left-pointing footpath sign indicates your path back along your outward route, passing to the rear of Manor Farm into the village and the Hoddington Arms.

Through the 'Lyths and Hangers' around Selborne

WALK 18

Allow 2 $^1/_2$ hours
4 $^1/_2$ miles

Walk begins page 109

Background to the walk

The charming village of Selborne is renowned throughout the world as the birthplace and home of Gilbert White, our country's most famous pioneer naturalist. The book which made White and Selborne famous is 'The Natural History and Antiquities of Selborne', published in 1789, and based on 40 years observation of wildlife in the garden of his home 'The Wakes' and around the village. The landscape around Selborne has changed little since his time and happily much of it is now preserved by the National Trust. The Wakes, where White lived from 1730 until his death in 1793 now houses two museums; the ground floor dedicated to the life and work of the naturalist and the Oates Museum on the first floor, which commemorates Francis Oates, the explorer of South America and Africa, and his nephew Captain Lawrence Oates, who accompanied Scott on the ill-fated expedition to the South Pole in 1911-12.

White is buried in St Mary's churchyard, the simple gravestone being inscribed with 'GW' and his dates. The church was built around 1180 on the site of the original Saxon church. Features of interest include White's memorial window depicting St Francis of Assisi preaching to 82 birds, all of which are mentioned in his book and a Flemish painting of about 1510. Just inside the churchyard entrance is the trunk of a yew tree, estimated to be about 1400 years old. By 1990 it measured 26 feet in girth and was taller than the church

Maps
Landranger 1:50,000
Sheet 186. Pathfinder
1:25,000 Sheet SU 63/
73. Map Reference of
Start/Finish
SU742337.

How to get there
From Winchester head
east via B3404 and
A31 for Alton and
Farnham, by-passing
Alresford and passing
through Four Marks. At
the first roundabout
beyond Four Marks
take the 3rd exit and
pass through Chawton,
then turn right onto the
B3006 for Selborne,
turn right for the
National Trust car
park, just beyond the
Selborne Arms. Alder
Valley and Oakley
Coach services 214/
215 between Winches-
ter and Guildford, stop
in Alton where you
connect with service
202 between Alton and
Petersfield which stops
outside the Selborne
Arms (Monday to
Saturdays only). From

Basingstoke follow the A339 to Alton, turning right on the outskirts following 'superstore' sign. Pass beneath railway bridge and go across the roundabout beyond to join the B3006 for Selborne. Alder Valley Coach service 207 between Basingstoke and Farnham calls at Alton (Mondays to Saturdays only). Connect here with service 202 for Selborne.

Pub facilities
Selborne Arms
The comfortably furnished and characterful 'zig-zag' bar and the 'Hanger' bar are named after the well-known foot-paths made famous by Gilbert White and reached from behind the pub. Generous portions of bar food are served from 1200-1400 and from 1900-2100, the menu ranging from pies, steaks, fish, excellent jacket pota-toes, ploughmans, toasted sandwiches and pizzas. Children have their own menu and are welcome in the dining area. The sheltered garden has a Wendy house, swings and an aviary. Four real ales are kept — Courage Directors,

tower, but the great gale blew it down on January 25th, splitting the trunk in two.

The open space in front of the church is known as The Plestor, a name derived from 'playstow', which in the Middle Ages was a playground. Near the seat commemorating the coronation of King George VI is the site where the stocks and whip-ping post used to stand. They were removed by an unknown villager in 1750 and never found, despite a reward being offered. Just along the road from The Plestor and situated opposite The Wakes is the old butchers shop. It is hidden by two of the four original lime trees, planted by Gilbert White in 1756 to hide 'the blood and filth' from view as he worked in his parlour.

Selborne is also home to the first gypsy mu-seum in England — The Romany Folklore Museum. Situated in Limes End Yard it has traditional Romany living wagons and an exhibition of gypsy history, crafts and wagon-building with many details and documents relating to the history of gypsies. For those interested in rural relics, the Mallinson Collection at the Selborne Cottage Shop is worth a visit. Housed in a timbered barn-like room are various old agricultural tools, domestic bygones and a display featuring the old grocers shop 'Maxwells', which traded in Selborne from 1832-1949. The Cottage Shop next door is a bookshop selling natural history and country books — country writers, crafts and bygones — and is well worth a visit.

Our walk passes Priory Farm which stands on the site of Selborne Priory, founded in 1232 as a house of Augustinian Canons by Peter des Roches. The priory fell into ruin and many stones were carried off by villagers to repair their houses. It is said by some to be haunted.

Entering NT land from the church

Best, Wadworth 6X
and Marstons Pedigree
— and can be sampled
from 1100-1500 and
from 1730-2300.
Parties of walkers
catered for with prior
notice.

Queens Arms

There has been an inn
on this site since 1340,
the present building
dating from the early
1800's. It has 6 bed-
rooms, a restaurant,
large public bar and a
simply furnished
lounge bar. A black-
board menu is avail-
able daily from 1230-
1430 and from 1900-
2100, the short range
of dishes include at
least two soups —
cauliflower and stilton
and carrot and orange
on our visit — chicken
creole, Hungarian
goulash, mixed nut
casserole and
moussaka.
'Ploughpersons' include
cockles and mussels as
well as cheese. The bar
opens from 1130-1500
and from 1800-2300
with the usual Sunday
hours.

Walk 18.

Distance: *Allow two-and-a-half hours for this four-and-a-half mile walk, longer if you plan to explore Selborne and visit The Wakes.*

We parked in the (free) National Trust car park behind the Selborne Arms before setting off north along the footway beside the B3006 into the village centre. Pass the Queens Arms on your right, then pass the Mallinson Collection of rural relics and The Wakes prior to crossing the busy road onto 'The Plestor' or village green and St Mary's Church. Beside the green a fingerpost indicates that you are on the 'Hangers Way' footpath and directs you across the attractive cottage-lined green, passing a large bench-surrounded oak tree to a metal gate in the churchyard wall. St Mary's church is worth a visit to see the memorials to the White family and to view Gilbert Whites grave, which is arrowed from your path as you cross the churchyard.

Beyond a wooden swing gate enter National Trust land — Church Meadow — with views across the 'lyths' or meadows into the valley and Oakhanger Stream. Bear half-right towards a stone cottage and a stile in the hedge to a narrow lane. Follow the lane downhill to pass the magnificent cottage known as Dortons. This rambling 17th century, long mullioned cottage, has herringbone brickwork above its porches and is located beside the stream. Your metalled lane soon gives way to a stony and often muddy track passing to the right of a row of poplar trees, before rising gently to become lined with mature trees.

Your route shortly bears left into Great Dorton Wood, parallel to Oakhanger Stream with the poplar-filled Long Lythe beyond. As we strolled through these tranquil pockets of beech trees, observing the abundant bird and animal life, we could begin to understand how Gilbert White loved to walk these paths, cherishing and recording all the beauty that he could see around him. The landscape around Selborne has always been praised for its beauty; in 1823 William Cobbett said 'nothing could surpass these dells and hillocks and hangers'. Eventually, at the end of the wood, climb the stile flanking a wooden gate and enter a pasture. A yellow arrow waymarks you along a defined grassy track, following the right-hand edge of the pasture. Cross a metal stile beside a gate and proceed ahead with the yellow arrow to another stile and wooden gate, joining a hedged trackway towards Priory Farm, which is built on the site of Selborne Priory. Pass a couple of cottages to your right before merging with the farm approach road.

In a little way climb the stile on your left, cross a small footbridge over the stream and follow the established path through scrub and pasture, to the stile preceding the woodland ahead. Beyond the stile, disregard the narrow arrowed path left and the stile across your track, instead bear left uphill, along the wide, tree-canopied cobbled lane into Coombe Wood. Gently ascend, bearing right through the predominantly hazel and oak wood until you reach a fork in the track. Here you veer left towards a green gate and stile at the woodland edge and enter lush pasture. From your elevated position there are fine views back to the heavily wooded Hangers high above Selborne.

Proceed straight on through the pasture, along a line of oak trees to where you pick up a more defined trackway, which soon veers sharp right uphill affording open vistas south-east into West Sussex and the South Downs. When you reach two gates, a fingerpost points your way through the right-hand gate, onto a bridleway that passes between an oak-lined hawthorn hedgerow and a wire fence. This old partly sunken routeway leads you to Wick Hill Farm where you pass to the right of the farmhouse, ignoring the arrowed footpath right, to follow the pitted drive northwards. Where the metalled lane bears right, turn left at the bridleway fingerpost onto a grass centred stony track, which shortly passes to the left of a magnificent thatched cottage — Wick Hill Cottages. The well-maintained grassy path soon gives way to an established track, following the edge of Long Copse and Milking Hanger to an oak tree and footpath sign located at the end of the trees.

Your route now bears right-handed along a wire fence, shortly joining a

Walk 18

NOTE
THIS MAP IS DIAGRAMMATIC
ONLY AND IS NOT TO SCALE

HARTLEY PARK FARM

B 3006

WICK HILL HANGER

WICK HILL COTTAGES

NORTON FARM

WICK HILL FARM

LONG COPSE

WICK WOOD

OAKHANGER STREAM

COOMBE WOOD

PRIORY FARM

GRANGE FARM

LONG LYTHE

HANGERS WAY

DORTON WOOD

THE WAKES

NEW BARN FARM

SELBORNE

2

1

CAR PARK

SELBORNE HANGER

SELBORNE COMMON

SELBORNE HILL

KETCHER'S FARM

B 3006

GALLEY HILL

KEY

- - - FOOTPATH

===== TRACK

⎯⎯ METALLED ROAD

✛ CHURCH

▢ GENERALISED BUILDING

➡ ROUTE OF WALK

✳ START POINT

PUBLIC HOUSES
(SHOWN BY A CIRCLE)

1 ⎯ SELBORNE ARMS

2 ⎯ QUEENS HOTEL

Selborne from the Hangers

grassy track at a metal gate. With good views to your left to the beech hangers towering over the surrounding fields, maintain your westerly course along varying track surfaces — some quite muddy — to the B3006. Taking care, cross this busy road, pass through a gate to where your path is waymarked along the right-hand edge of an arable field. Still walking westwards, follow the field edge round to the left, shortly to bear right at the yellow arrow, to pass between two old fence posts and cross a wooden bridge over a drainage channel. A defined path then takes you across a field to a stile located in the hedgerow. Climb the stile and the one immediately to your left, then head straight across the pasture to a gap in the hedgerow and enter a further pasture. Follow the hedge right-handed, with Selborne visible to your left, down to a stile and a gate. A hedged trackway beyond leads you down to a lane — Gracious Street — where you turn left for a short distance, to a right-pointing fingerpost located just past the first cottage on your right.

This metalled drive passes 'Fisher's Lodge' and soon becomes a muddy thoroughfare, which bears left, gradually rising uphill. Disregard the footpath waymarked over a stile on your left and proceed along your path to a National Trust sign notifying you that you are now on Selborne Common. Your route now turns left rising sharply uphill via an established track into beech woodland, known as 'The Hangers'. Do not take the sunken pathway, but keep to the muddy path to its left. This pathway passes beneath a thick canopy of old beech trees — many over 300 years old — with occasional cameo views down into Selborne and beyond into East Hampshire. The Hanger is a steep scarp face of chalk rising 300 feet above the village. Where the path forks, keep left to a metal seat and pause for a while here to absorb the famous tree-fringed view across the village and the peace and quiet around you. Pass through a walk-through stile onto a gravel path — The Bostal Path — which descends the scarp face down to a NT donation collection pillar and kissing gate. It is here that the 'Zig-Zag' route begins its ascent of the Hangers. This path was created by Gilbert White and his brother in 1753 as a short cut to the Hanger. Pass through the kissing gate and follow the wide stony path back to the car park behind the Selborne Arms.

Downland ways around Priors Dean from *The White Horse*

Background to the walk

The White Horse is one of the highest and most isolated public houses in Hampshire, set high up on Froxfield plateau. It lies sheltered by a clump of trees, in the middle of fields at the end of a rough track off one of the minor roads that cross this lonely countryside. As an inn it dates from 1620, when an old road from Alton to Petersfield, through East Tisted and Colemore, came across the plateau past the inn. The inn is also known as the 'Pub with No Name' for their is no sign announcing its presence, only an old wooden cradle exists, the sign having been stolen some years ago.

As well as being a classic example of a totally unspoilt country pub, the inn was once a favourite haunt of the poet Edward Thomas in the early years of this century, and his tankard still hangs in the bar! The White Horse inspired his first poem 'Up in the Wind' (1914), in which he describes the inn's isolation. Edward Thomas lived in the nearby villages of Steep and Froxfield, before his untimely death during the First World War, in the Battle of Arras in 1917, at the age of 39.

The tiny hamlet of Priors Dean lies just off our walk, but it is well worth the short diversion and stroll down the lane, to view the old church and manor. It nestles in a valley, high up in chalk countryside and has changed little since 1900, comprising a church, an ancient yew — thought to be over a thousand years old — a farm, a manor and a few cottages. It came to be called 'Priors Dean' because it once belonged to Southwick

Maps
Landranger 1:50,000 Sheet 186. Pathfinder 1:25,000 Sheets SU 63/73 and SU 62/72 Map Reference of Start/Finish SU715290.

How to get there

From Winchester head east from King Alfred's statue following signs for Petersfield (A272). Cross the motorway, then at the roundabout take the 3rd exit, then shortly bear off left onto the A272 for Petersfield. Follow this for 9 miles to the traffic lights and junction with the A32. Turn left here towards Alton for three-and-a-half miles before turning right signposted Steep. Take the third turning on your left after nearly 2 miles, looking out for the empty pub sign cradle. The White Horse lies along the second track on your right. From Basingstoke follow the

A339 south to Alton,
then follow the A32
signs through the town,
picking up the road
south west of the town.
Pass through East
Tisted, then take the
2nd turning on your left
for Steep — follow
Winchester directions
from here.

Pub facilities
The White Horse
(pictured right)
Country pub enthusi-
asts drive miles to seek
out this 'timeless' rural
gem. Its two bars are
charmingly rustic,
unspoilt by modernity
and with a relaxed
atmosphere. Winter log
fires are fronted with
rocking chairs or an old
sofa and both bars are
simply furnished with
an array of antique
furniture — old settles,
drop-leaf tables and a
grandfather clock —
old pictures, farm
implements and rugs.
The unpretentious
character of the pub is
matched by the hearty
snacks that are served
daily from 1200-1400
(sandwiches only
Sunday) and Wednes-
day to Saturday
evenings from 1930-
2130. In winter, thick
warming soup is
popular — other dishes
include cottage pie,
steak and kidney pie,

Priory. The tiny church is 13th and 14th century, but is entered by a Norman doorway. It was restored in 1856 and various internal fittings date from that time, although of note are the floor brasses dating from 1605 and four wall monuments to the Compton family dated 1653. The floor of the manor has yielded many thrilling finds — two toy lead cups and saucers, a Stuart stirrup-iron and a clip thought to be the top of a chatelaine.

Colemore, is another tiny rural collection of houses, a farm and a manor, centred around the picturesque little church of St Peter ad Vincula. The first recorded mention of Colemore was in Domesday in 1086, though there is evidence in local place-names that there was a Saxon settlement in the area and there has been a church on the site since the 10th century. The church that stands today is Norman and it is unusual for such a small church to have transepts. Also of interest is the Norman purple marble font and a ladder in the west end that date from 1694. The church is beautifully maintained by the Redundant Churches Fund and is open for people to view its tranquil interior.

lasagne, ploughmans, salads and a range of sandwiches. Up to a dozen excellent real ales — Ballards, Ringwood, Gales, King and Barnes, Eldridge Pope — and a range of country wines can be sampled between 1100 and 1430 (1500 on Saturdays) and from 1800-2300. Usual hours on Sundays. Children not allowed in the bars, but there is an outdoor play area in the large garden. There are facilities in the nearby field for cara-vans.

Walk 19.

Distance: *Allow at least three hours for this six mile walk.*

Having found this wonderful atmospheric pub, you will be very reluctant to disturb the pub cat that has probably curled up on your lap, during the time you have been relaxing in the rocking chair, warming your toes in front of the roaring log fire — especially if the weather is inclement!

But it's 3pm and the door has been bolted behind you, so cross the car park and pass through the field entrance opposite the pond. Once in the field turn right, to follow the car park fence to a stile in the far hedge. Climb the stile, then proceed straight across an arable field — striding out having realised that you should be back in the car park as the bolt on the pub door slides open at 6pm! — towards a low shed ahead of you. A fingerpost soon directs you along its perimeter fence, through a gap in the hedgerow, where you follow the field edge right-handed. Maintain your course round the field passing a huge metal storage barn and a garage complex on your right. Shortly, leave the hedge to follow a visible path half-left across the arable field, towards two trees and a red-roofed house. On nearing the house you are waymarked along a hedge, your path affords open views north across rolling Hamp-shire countryside.

When you reach a green painted gate, either cross the stile — broken on our visit — to its right or pass to the left of the gate to a lane. Cross the lane to join Warren Lane, which you follow downhill passing Langley Stables on your left. This dead-end lane is quiet, thickly hedged, with the occasional rural cameo view to your left and right. Pass 'The Forge' and progress downhill to a garage with a green door, which lies to your right. Here you proceed straight on, joining a track at the 'Unfit for Motors' sign, which shortly gives way to a narrow old routeway, just beyond a partly-thatched cottage. Pinned to its white gates — when we passed by — was a polythene-covered piece of paper with the following verse written on it — 'What would the world be, once bereft of wet and wildness? Let them be left, O let them be left, wildness and wet; Long live the weeds and the wildness yet' (Gerald Manley Hopkins). It is food for thought as our walk continues through some of the most beautiful countryside in Hampshire and one realises how susceptible our few wild and undisturbed areas are to man's dominance.

Now begin to descend a fine old high-banked routeway, lined with yew and beech and thick with mud after rain. Emerge from the leafy old lane to join a track to the left of an attractive brick house called 'Doscombe' and follow its gravel and concrete driveway to a metalled lane. Your route bears left along this narrow, peaceful hedged lane which is surrounded by wooded hills. Just beyond the 1:5 hill sign and the second passing place on your left, lookout for the fingerpost pointing your way left, up a bank into a field. Keep ahead, your path following the line of an overhanging beech wood. Enjoy fine views west, across the Rother Valley towards Liss.

When you reach the edge of the wood, proceed across a short stretch of cropland to a fingerpost just visible in the trees beyond, which directs you uphill along a narrow wooded path. At the top of the hill, leave the wood via a stile and maintain your uphill course along the right-hand fence of a pasture. When you reach a stile to your right, just before a wooden gate, pause and admire the panorama that has unfolded behind you. Climb the stile, following the path within a thick hedgerow to a further stile, where you bear left uphill along an old sunken tree-lined track to a narrow lane. Turn right here and follow the lane downhill to visit Priors Dean.

Our main route bears left at the crest of the hill, along another quiet lane to Five Ash Farm. Bear right to follow the tarmac drive to the rear of a couple of bungalows, before it gives way to a trackway leading you to a series of farm buildings. Remain on the track, which in turn becomes a grassy green lane passing between mature tree-lined hedges, beyond the barns. Shortly, this narrows down to a muddy track where a significant tree canopy envelopes the thoroughfare, as you progress to a metalled lane. Unfortunately, the rapidly disappearing old-style metal fingerpost, which should have arrowed your route across the lane and along a leafy, coppice-lined lane towards Colemore, lay broken on the verge.

Where this peaceful little lane bears left, veer off right with the footpath sign and cross a stile into a field. A further left-pointing fingerpost, near some old farm machinery ahead, directs you through a field entrance and along a wire fence, to where a yellow arrow indicates your route half-right across the pasture to a stile in the corner. Beyond the stile, follow the hedge right-handed, climb a further nettled stile, then proceed on the same course through brambly rough pasture to another stile in the far right-hand corner. Turn left then left again to follow the field edge uphill, with woodland to your left. Where two woods meet, your path — which can be quite overgrown — bears left through the trees into a field beyond. Here you keep left, uphill for a few yards along a grassy track before leaving the woodland edge where it curves left, to join a visible path through a crop field, passing a telegraph pole to a lane.

With open arable views westwards, cross the lane onto a waymarked track towards the hamlet of Colemore in front of you. Turn left when you

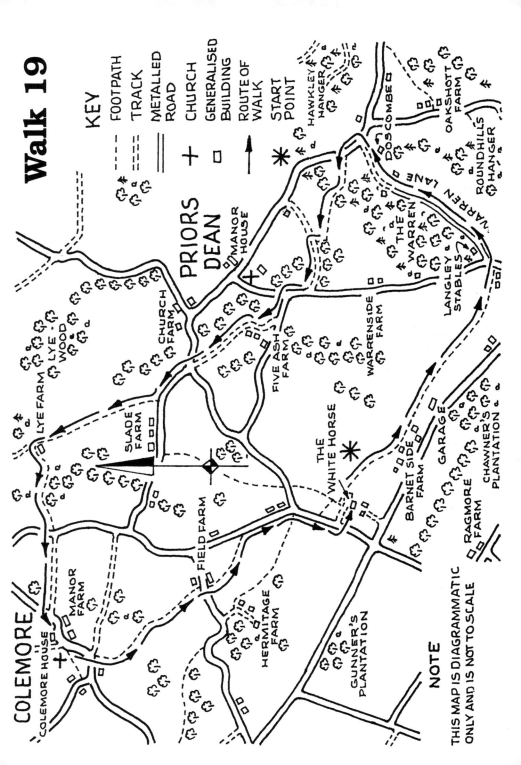

reach another lane, following it through the tiny group of houses, passing Colemore House and Manor Farm to the Norman church of St Peter ad Vincula. Remain on the lane, disregarding the fingerpost and stile to your right just beyond the church, to where the lane bears right. Here you veer left along a grass track to a fingerpost, which points your way uphill along a grassy patch between two crop fields. Keep to the left-hand side of a line of trees, following the field edge to a gap in the hedge on your right.

A large field presents itself, through which you bear half-left aiming for the stile visible at the end of some trees, to the right of a house. The field contained remnants of old crops which made the going tough and tiring as we gradually climbed uphill to the stile. Once over the stile, the views back across open countryside made the effort seem worthwhile. With grass underfoot now proceed across the pasture to a further stile, this time in the hedge in front of you. Drop down onto a lane and cross over near the pond at a fingerpost, which arrows your route across a stile into a paddock. Bear half-left to another stile, then maintain direction through a further paddock to a double stile. Cross the field ahead towards a group of three telegraph poles and pass through the metal gates beyond, bearing right along a narrow country lane. Keep right at the next junction, then lookout for a stile in the hedge to your left, beyond which you follow the hedge right-handed to another stile on your right. The White Horse is immediately ahead of you, across the field.

A woodland walk from *The Harrow* near Steep

Background to the walk

Steep is an area of scattered farms and a few large houses nestling on the lower slopes of a wooded chalk escarpment that forms the western edge of the Weald. Stoner, Shoulder of Mutton and Wheatham hills form the beech and yew-covered ridge that twists and writhes through Steep and Oakshott, affording magnificent views, on a clear day, along the length of the South Downs, as far as Devil's Dyke and Ditchling Beacon. The area has long been known as Little Switzerland for its quite unique scenery. Long before a well-engineered zig-zag road was constructed up 'Lutcombe' in the 1820s, horse-drawn coaches had to labour up a gruelling steep and stony track that climbed the face of Stoner Hill. This historic coaching route linked Petersfield with Alton, Winchester and the Midlands.

One of Britain's most celebrated public schools, Bedales, moved to Steep in 1900, establishing the first progressive co-educational public school in England at the time. The presence of the school stimulated the growth of the village, creating a main street, a village shop and post office and gave employment to people in the area. The school also attracted the promising poet, Edward Thomas and his family to the village in 1906, so that his children could attend the school. The wooded heights, mysterious combes and sheer beauty of the local landscape inspired Thomas to write poetry, and most of his material refers to the years he spent in Steep.

Maps
Landranger 1:50,000 Sheet 197. Pathfinder 1:25,000 Sheet SU 62/ 72 Map Reference of Start/Finish SU751251

How to get there
From Winchester head east from King Alfred's statue following signs for Petersfield (A272). Cross the motorway then at the roundabout take the third exit, then shortly bear off left onto the A272 for Petersfield. Follow this for 15 miles to the small roundabout on the edge of town and take the first exit signed to Steep. Turn right at the Cricketers pub, following the lane past the church and on for a further mile to the Harrow. From Basingstoke follow the A339 south to Alton then follow the A32 signs through the town, picking up the road south-west of the town. Pass through East Tistead then take the

2nd turning on your left for Steep, follow the road to the Cricketers pub and turn left.

Pub facilities
The Harrow
(pictured right)
Tucked away down small country lanes The Harrow is another gem of a rustic pub, still totally unspoilt and with a charming old-fashioned atmosphere, rarely found today. Two small bars have boarded walls and are simply furnished, the left-hand bar with built-in wall benches around scrubbed deal tables on a tiled floor, a huge inglenook and shelves of old books. Both bars are festooned with seasonal wild flower and fruit arrange-ments. From two serving hatches you can request a pint of Strongs Country Bitter, Boddingtons Bitter and Flowers Original, all tapped straight from the cask or you can order a hearty home-made snack from the short and simple menu. Generous portions of tasty country soup overflow from large china bowls and are accompanied by home-baked bread, ploughmans and salads featuring ham,

The Thomases lived in three houses in the village between 1906 and his untimely death in the First World War in 1917. Berryfield Cottage was the poet's first home, located next to a large manor, Ashford Chace, at the base of his beloved hangers and passed on this walk. The family then moved to The Red House, a fine residence on Cockshott Lane, high up on the chalk escarpment among the beech hangers. Thomas enjoyed the four years they spent there and his poems 'The New House' and 'Wind and Mist' refer to this house — 'We lived in clouds, on a cliff's edge'. Their final home was in the village at No.2 Yew Tree Cottages, during which time he wrote the majority of his work.

Two memorials exist in the area, commemo-rating the poet's life and work; the first a sarsen stone dedicated to his memory, erected in 1937 on Shoulder of Mutton Hill, a favourite spot of his from which magnificent views unfold of 'sixty miles of South Downs at one glance' as Thomas described it. The partly-Norman church of All Saints contains two small lancet windows designed and engraved by Laurence Whistler and installed in 1978 on the centenary of Thomas's birth.

Other features of note in the church are the kneelers, depicting different rural scenes and plants and animals. A great number of these were designed by the vicar and embroidered by the ladies of the parish.

The hangers are drained by the River Ashford which was once powerful enough to drive a fulling mill and later a grain mill. The old mill and waterfall is now a popular beauty spot and our route passes the site towards the end of the walk.

Walk 20.

Distance: *Allow three hours for this six mile walk.*

From the rustic and traditional confines of the Harrow turn left along the matalled lane, passing the parking area for the pub, then in a short distance at a pair of wooden gates bear left onto a footbridge which leads you across the idly flowing River Ashford — a tributary of the Rother — to an area known as Kettlebrook. Your path curves left in front of an attractive thatched cottage, shortly to bear right along the edge of a mixed woodland with an old deep, sunken, beech-lined lane to your left. This water-filled gully was once the route of a 10th century road which linked Petersfield to Liss. The earth path soon brings you to a narrow macadamised lane which you follow north, gently rising uphill to pass a dwelling named 'Natterjacks', before you turn left at the footpath fingerpost arrowing your route along a stony track.

In a little way climb the stile in the fence to your left into pasture and follow the fence right-handed, with the immense bulk of Wheatham Hill now clearly visible northwards. A yellow arrow directs you around the field edge to a further stile that precedes a woodland. Beyond this a narrow path leads you along the right-hand edge of a conifer plantation, steeply downhill to a broken stile, where you pass to its left to a junction of three routes. Turn right here with the fingerpost and pass through an old gateway onto a defined path that follows a mature woodland edge to a stile. Enter the woodland, your stony path crossing a small brook before emerging from the trees to cross the edge of a garden belonging to a white-painted cottage. Follow the white footpath signs over the driveway between the garage and house and re-enter the mixed woodland.

Eventually your path rises to a concrete area and huge battery chicken shed. Keep ahead towards the three-arrowed fingerpost, shortly leaving the concrete to bear left across a small wooden footbridge to a stile. Once over the stile follow the field edge right-handed along a line of trees to the corner where you keep right to another stile at the woodland fringe.

rare roast beef, scotch egg and cheeses with home-made pickle. Hot dishes include lasagne, quiche or baked marrow. Food is served from 1200-1345 and 1830-2200 and the bar from 1100-1430 and 1800-2300, usual hours Sunday. There is a long flower-filled garden and patio for fine weather eating and drinking. Children are not allowed in the pub.

Riverside cottage, Steep

Proceed along the woodland border to climb a second stile into lush pasture and bear half-left, keeping just to the left of the line of telegraph poles. A yellow arrow on the second pole points your way left towards the stile flanking a metal gate, beyond which you climb uphill along a narrow grassy path to a lane located at the base of the hangers and turn right.

Follow the lane to where a further lane enters from your right then look out for a waymarked footpath over a stile to your left that takes you into pasture. Proceed ahead, uphill along two lines of trees to a stile at a woodland boundary. Beyond the stile bear left onto an old muddy and slippery thoroughfare that climbs steadily uphill through the magnificent beech hangers to the summit of Wheatham Hill. The track forms part of the established walk 'The Hangers Way' which links Selborne and Steep — at this point views begin to unfold southwards across Petersfield to the South Downs. The long energy-sapping climb begins to level out towards the top passing between yew and beech to where a wide trackway joins your route from the right. Turn right here, then in a short distance pause at a gateway on your left and absorb the cameo view that presents itself, across rolling Hampshire countryside.

The old droving trackway soon bears right downhill, becoming steep-sided and passing beneath a fine canopy of beech trees, this time affording splendid views across the Rother valley towards Liss. Nearing the bottom of the hill your route becomes rutted, then bears right to join a tiny lane beside the entrance to Wheatham Hill House. Bear right for a little way, before veering left at the sharp right-hand bend onto a waymarked hedged right of way. When you reach a left-pointing fingerpost double back slightly along the hedge to where a yellow arrow directs you along a grassy path, between a wire fence and scrubland. Follow the fence right with views towards the unusual tower of Hawkley church peering above the trees, and away to your right to the wooded hills beyond Liss.

Gradually descend and cross a stile, then head downhill along the field edge beside a wood into Oakshott valley. Once in the base of the valley

climb a stile in the fence on your right and enter the copse, shortly crossing a small footbridge over Oakshott Stream to another stile. In the meadow beyond follow the defined grassy path to the right of a wooden shed, then rise uphill to where a fingerpost points your route left, along a scenic path through wild meadowland, abundant with wild flowers and wildlife. Your route follows the valley bottom, crossing two stiles before skirting the edge of a beech wood, along what can be a nettle infested path to a plank bridge and stile. Unspoilt country scenes and wildlife surround you along this truly peaceful stretch of the walk — we saw a kestrel, magpies, nuthatches, a green woodpecker, finches and numerous species of butterflies as we passed this idyllic valley.

Beyond the stile, cross lush pasture to a further plank bridge over Oakshott Stream, climb the stile ahead and turn right to follow the path along the valley side, just above the stream. Keep to this narrow stretch of sheep grazed pasture to a stile, a lane and splendid brick and timber barn. Cross the lane to where a Wayfarers Walk fingerpost — Petersfield and Steep — waymarks your route up a stony track leading to Lower Oakshott House. Pass Neals Cottage on your right, then pass through a wooden gate onto a gravel driveway, shortly to bear left round the garden of Lower Oakshott House on a narrow grassy pathway and begin your long climb back up Wheatham Hill.

In a short distance climb a stile into a lush and very steep meadow. Wild flowers seem to flourish on this grassland, in particular cowslips, which carpet the hillside in yellow in early spring. Slowly ascend this arduous climb, frequently pausing to catch you breath and to take in the panoramic views that rapidly unfold behind you. Cross the stile at the edge of the meadow and enter beech woodland, your path still rising uphill to another stile and a fingerpost announcing that you are back on the Hangers Way. Maintain your energy-sapping haul up Wheatham Hill through glorious beech hangers, keeping right along the fence on emerging from the trees, shortly reaching the top of the hill and the main muddy summit thorough-fare beyond a stile. Turn right, then in a little way bear left at the Hangers Way fingerpost onto a defined pathway through the trees, then through two walk-through stiles and begin to descend Shoulder of Mutton Hill

Soon the memorial stone to the poet Edward Thomas comes into view, as does the superb vista across Steep and the South Downs, a view Thomas cherished dearly and expresses in many of his poems. The plaque on the stone is inscribed with the following very apt line from one of his poems — 'and I rose up and knew I was tired and continued my journey' — for legs are probably weary by now as you near the end of the walk. Luck has it, for some kind soul has placed a seat just below the stone, perfect for resting tired limbs and absorbing the stunning rural scene that lies in front of you.

Your route now descends the very steep scarp slope (care to be taken)

Thomas memorial on Shoulder of Mutton Hill

on a wide grassy thoroughfare flanked on either side with beech and yew. Wooden steps cut into the hill aid your descent near the bottom prior to you reaching a stile, beyond which you follow the right-hand edge of a crop field to a lane. Turn right here towards a large building — Ashford Chace — and the adjacent Berryfield Cottage, the first home of Edward Thomas during his years in the village. Just before the house cross the stile on your left, a fingerpost points you along a grass-centred track which follows the edge of the garden to Ashford Chace. Shortly, veer off left onto a footpath to a stile and enter a woodland. This peaceful woodland way bears right then left to run parallel with the River Ashford and its small lake before it forks. Here you bear right onto a narrow path, downhill to a lane and the Old Mill, with the waterfall which once powered the mill to your right.

Turn right along the lane, shortly take the waymarked path opposite a junction of lanes. Pass through a metal kissing gate and proceed straight across the pasture ahead, keeping close to the woodland to a plank aiding your route across a boggy area and a stile. A stony path now leads you uphill through beech woods, soon to emerge into a bracken area before crossing a small playing field to a lane and All Saints church in Steep. Your route bears left, then follows the lane right, downhill back to The Harrow and your car.

· BIBLIOGRAPHY ·

As this is predominantly a walking book, space for in-depth research and writing on the history of the villages and places of interest passed on the walks has been somewhat limited. As well as gleaning information from various church leaflets, from the landlords and other local characters met on route, the following source material has been used in the preparation of this book:

Along and Around the Wayfarers Walk. Hampshire Recreation.

The Edward Thomas Country. W. M. Whiteman, Paul Cave Publications.

Hampshire, The Complete Guide. Jo Draper, Dovecote Press.

Hampshire Curiosities. Jo Draper, Dovecote Press.

Hampshire with the Isle of Wight. Ed. Arthur Mee, Hodder and Stoughton.

Hidden Hampshire. John Barton, Countryside Books.

It Happened in Hampshire. Hampshire Women's Institutes.

The New Hampshire Village Book. Hampshire Women's Institutes.

A Picture of Hampshire. John Baker, Robert Hale.

Pub Walks around Portsmouth. John Price, Ensign Publications.

Pub Walks around Southampton. Peter Carne, Ensign Publications.

Pub Walks in the New Forest. Diana Smith, Ensign Publications.

This Village of Greywell. Anne Pitcher, Bird Brothers.

Visitors Guide to Hampshire & the Isle of Wight. John Barton, Moorland.

· ACKNOWLEDGEMENTS ·

I would like to thank the following people, without them this book may not have been written.

In compiling this collection of walks I am deeply indebted to the contribution of my friend and colleague Bonita Toms; without her encouragement and support I would not have written this book. Bonita accompanied me on all the walks, took all the photographs, made invaluable observations and notes on each walk and showed exemplary patience during the many hours I have spent on the project over the last few months.

I am grateful to another friend and colleague Allen Stidwill for making time in his busy schedule to read the walks copy.

I thank Jack Street, who is responsible for preparing the excellent sketch-maps that accompany each walk description.

I acknowledge John Price and Peter Carne who wrote the preceding volumes in this series — *Pub Walks around Portsmouth and the South Downs* and *Pub Walks around Southampton and Central Hampshire* — both have set a good style to which I was able to refer.

Finally, I am grateful to the landlords of the pubs mentioned, for their cooperation and more importantly for the enthusiasm they expressed in the concept of Pub Walks.

· INDEX OF PUBS ·